KING OF ENGLAND & BASTARD ANGEL

When Mr King retires after thirty-five years as
in East London, he celebrates the occasion by
at a smart West End restaurant. It should be a
that he has in store for Linda and Susan backfi
never forget.

King of England was premièred at the Theatre Royal, Stratford East in 1988, and
Rudolph Walker won a *Time Out/01 for London* Award for his outstanding
performance as Mr King.

Bastard Angel focuses on an enduring female rock star. Intercut with sections of a
Berlin concert during a European tour, the four-act play is concerned with singer
Shelly's assessment of her decade and a half as leader of a world famous rock band.

Bastard Angel was premièred by the Royal Shakespeare Company at the Warehouse,
London in 1980.

BARRIE KEEFFE was born in East London in 1945. His plays include *Only a Game*
(Shaw Theatre, 1973), *Scribes* (Greenwich Theatre, 1976), *A Mad World, My
Masters* (for Joint Stock, 1977), *Frozen Assets* (RSC, 1978), *Bastard Angel* (RSC,
1980), *Better Times* (Theatre Royal, Stratford, East London, 1985), *King of England*
(Theatre Royal, Stratford East, 1988), and, for the National Youth Theatre of Great
Britain, *A Sight of Glory* (1975), *Here Comes the Sun* (1976), and *Up the Truncheon*
(1977). For the Soho Poly Theatre Club he has written *Sus* (1979; also seen at the
Royal Court) and two trilogies: *Gimme Shelter* (*Gem, Gotcha, Getaway*) also staged
at the Royal Court in 1977, and *Barbarians* (*Killing Time, Abide With Me, In the
City*) which played Greenwich in 1977. His work for TV includes *Nipper, Hanging
Around, Waterloo Sunset*, adaptations of *Gotcha, Gem* (retitled *Not Quite Cricket*),
Abide With Me (retitled *Champions*) and a serial, *No Excuses* (published in novel
form) based on his play, *Bastard Angel*. Keeffe was Thames TV Playwrights' Award
resident dramatist at the Shaw Theatre in 1977 and writer in residence with the RSC
in 1978. In 1979 *Gotcha* received the French theatre critics' Prix Revelation, and his
radio play *Heaven Scent* won a Giles Cooper Award. For the cinema he wrote the
screenplay for *The Long Good Friday* (1981), for which, in 1983, he won the Mystery
Writers of America Edgar Allen Poe Award.

*The photograph on the front cover is of West Indian immigrants arriving in Britain in
1956. Reproduced by kind permission of the BBC Hulton Picture Library.*

KING OF ENGLAND
&
BASTARD ANGEL

Two Plays by

BARRIE KEEFFE

METHUEN DRAMA

A METHUEN NEW THEATRESCRIPT

Bastard Angel first published in 1980 by Eyre Methuen Ltd.
King of England first published with *Bastard Angel* as a paperback original in Great Britain in 1988 by Methuen Drama, Michelin House, 81 Fulham Road, SW3 6RB and distributed in the United States of America by HEB Inc., 70 Court Street, Portsmouth, New Hampshire 03801.

British Library Cataloguing in Publication Data
Keeffe, Barrie, 1945–
   King of England & bastard angel. – (Methuen new theatrescripts).
   I. Title
   822'.914

ISBN 0 413 19320 9

Printed in Great Britain by Richard Clay Ltd, Bungay, Suffolk.

CAUTION
All rights whatsoever in these plays are strictly reserved and application for performance etc. should be made to Harvey Unna and Stephen Durbridge Ltd, 24 Pottery Lane, Holland Park, London W11 4LZ. No performance may be given unless a licence has been obtained.

Author's Preface

Both *King of England* and *Bastard Angel* have borrowed from other plays and appeared in different forms.

King Lear was the starting point for *King of England* after a chance meeting in a Post Office with a West Indian tube train driver, collecting his pension. I first wrote the play with the title *Black Lear*: it was toured by the Temba Theatre Company in 1980. Dissatisfied with it, I re-wrote it – using the same central character – as a short television play *King* which was transmitted by the BBC in 1984. *King of England* was a further re-working of the TV script, enlarging the play and introducing the character Jimmy.

I had been trying to write the play that became *Bastard Angel* for some time, but could find no satisfactory structure. The writing started after I saw a production of Chekhov's first full length play *Platonov* (as it is usually known) in Amsterdam in 1978. The play was performed in, for me, inpenetrable Dutch but this wasn't a handicap in that it allowed my imagination to run and I followed the settings and visual images – the firework party, the death on the railway, for example – in writing *Bastard Angel*. After the Royal Shakespeare Company's production in 1980, I began writing a companion piece *White Line Fever* which followed Shelley from the Berlin gig back to England and her past. I never completed the play, but instead wrote a seven part TV series for Central Television entitled *No Excuses*. This used *Bastard Angel* for the first four episodes and the material I had intended to use in *White Line Fever* for the remaining three. It was transmitted in the summer of 1983 and the scripts published in novel form, also called *No Excuses*.

The texts in this volume are the versions I prefer.

Barrie Keeffe, 1988

KING OF ENGLAND

For Stephen Durbridge

How sharper than a serpent's tooth it is
To have a thankless child.

King Lear, Act I, scene iv

King of England was first performed at the Theatre Royal, Stratford East on 28 January 1988, with the following cast:

MR KING Rudolph Walker
SUSAN Claire Benedict
LINDA Ellen Thomas
STEVIE Paul Barber
WAITER/JIMMY/
DOCTOR Larry Dann

Directed by Philip Hedley
Designed by Jackie Pilford and Jenny Tiramani
Lighting by Stephen Watson

ACT ONE
Scene One Mr King's house in Stratford
Scene Two A restaurant in Soho

ACT TWO
Scene One Stratford Railway Yard
Scene Two The local hospital, 1976
Scene Three Mr King's house in Stratford
Scene Four The local hospital, 1988

Music by Bob Marley
Before Play *I Am Going Home*
After Act One *No Woman No Cry*
Before Act Two *Time Will Tell*
After play/curtain *Redemption Song*

ACT ONE

Scene One

Music before play: Bob Marley's I am Going Home

KING *alone in spotlight on darkened stage.*

KING: Hey Malley . . . Oh Malley I wish you could be hearing me. I wish – I could be talking to you. Ooo, Malley, how I wish you could have been here with me today . . . at the depot. In the canteen this afternoon. That's where we had the party . . . in the canteen at the depot at Stratford Station. That's where Mister Cunningham made the retirement presentations – personally. Why I'm wearing the new suit. Red lining, too – like it?

He fiddles with watch on wrist and watch he pulls from his pocket.

I wore the watch you gave me . . . our 25th wedding anniversary. I had to take it off and put it in my pocket when I saw what . . . let me tell you Malley . . .

He steps forward, addresses audience – perhaps he'd been trying to spot MALLEY in the audience.

Three of my colleagues were also retiring. Bert and Donald and Mister Smythe . . . you may recall Mister Smythe who gave us such fear about his continuous stomach disorders . . . but now in tip top health, not what we feared. He's moving to a bungalow in Hastings . . . their wives were with them at the party . . . I wish you . . . you. (*Pause.*) A man from the London Transport Authority made a speech. A most unsuitable political speech, I thought, considering the occasion. I was given to understand he'd been a councillor for the GLC.

Mister Cunningham presented each of us with a watch. (*Holds it.*) This is the watch he presented me with. A six function digital watch . . . complete with alarm. The alarm plays The Yellow Rose of Texas. Wish I could ask you Malley . . . that what I'm gonna do tonight is right. I wish to Jesus that you hadn't died Malley . . .

and I wish you was going to be coming to the celebration tonight . . . and I wish, I wish . . . you were gonna be coming home with me . . . home to Trinidad.

Now full lights on to reveal KING's living room of small terraced house. There is a large trunk in the room. SUSAN enters wearing a nurse's uniform and carrying a bouquet of flowers.

Suzie . . . my Choosy, Choosy Suzie.

SUSAN: Hello dad.

KING: Suzie . . . you're here.

SUSAN: All these cards – all these Good Luck On Your Retirement cards . . . you got a lot of cards.

KING: So many. And now I got you here, Susan (*They hug.*)

SUSAN: What's this smell, dad? This smells . . . what is it?

KING: Oh the cologne you mean –

SUSAN: Yeah, the cologne –

KING: Some of the secretaries and typists and the office girls at the depot, they bought for me as a present . . . a bottle of manly cologne.

SUSAN: Manly cologne?

KING: You want to see the bottle?

SUSAN: No, no. Very manly.

KING: You like the smell? I wash it off if you don't like it.

SUSAN: There sure is a lot of it. (*Laughs.*)

KING: It was a special present from the ladies at the depot. For me. For the party, this afternoon in the canteen.

SUSAN: You sure got a lot of cards . . . and this . . .

She picks up scarf, vivid primary colours. KING lets her drape it round his neck.

KING: This afternoon was colleagues. Tonight is my family. You're here tonight, and that is what matters.

You like the scarf?

SUSAN: I like it, dad.

KING: She made it, Mrs Dwyer next

door. You remember Mrs Dwyer next door?

SUSAN: Of course I do.

KING: When Mrs Dwyer heard about I was retiring and going home . . . well, she knitted me this. As a present. For being a good neighbour, she said.

SUSAN: That's nice. I bought you some flowers. (*She can't quite hand them to him yet: he's at window, his back to her.*)

KING: She always asks after you girls. Did you wave at Mrs Dwyer's window when you comed in? 'Cause she's always at her window, waiting to wave at you girls.

SUSAN: Yeah, I saw her at the window, dad.

KING: She can't see too well now. She's almost blind now. It's amazing how she achieved such a colour combination of knitting the scarf. What are those things called that grow over old people's eyes?

SUSAN: Cateracts.

KING: That's what she's got. She's a remarkable knitter. What a scarf she knitted me, eh? (*Flaunts it.*) Back home, they'll have never seen a scarf like this one.

SUSAN: Just the kind of knitted scarf you need to wear in Trinidad, dad. When the temperature drops under ninety! (*She realises he is being serious. He keeps the scarf tied at neck.*)

KING: It can get cold there in the mornings. I'm going to worry about old Mrs Dwyer, how she's going to get on when I'm gone. I kept an eye on her – this neighbourhood not like what it used to be. She an old lady, and so many foreigners in the street now. Who'll keep an eye on old Mrs Dwyer when I go? (*Pause. SUSAN can't answer this.*)

SUSAN: When is it you go Dad, still Wednesday?

KING: Wednesday, yes. They come to take the trunk on Monday . . . then on Wednesday I fly.

SUSAN: So, it's all definite now?

KING: I fly on Wednesday.

SUSAN: I was hoping you might have had second thoughts, dad.

KING: It's what I always intended.

SUSAN: What I meant was –

KING: I have discussed this with you.

SUSAN: But what I meant was –

KING: So on Wednesday –

SUSAN: But in the same week, dad. Retiring, then uprooting and going to Trinidad in the same week? Well, I wish you weren't doing it all at once, dad.

KING: It's all decided. It's settled. Finito.

SUSAN: What about the house, I mean, what about –

KING: All in good time. Now come and give your daddy a great big kiss, because tonight Suzie – tonight is going to be the best damned night you had out in years. You can't wear that. You got a dress?

SUSAN: I just came from the hospital dad. Of course I brought a dress. Where are we going tonight then – all this mystery?

KING: You'll see, you'll see. It's all booked, it's all arranged. Just about the best damned restaurant in London. When I went to book the table last week, just the smell of the cooking in there nearly drove me crazy. We got a corner table. The manager personally advised me to hire it. It's hidden from the other clientele behind a kind of pillar. Very private. That's why you gotta dress up.

SUSAN (*takes dress from carrier bag*): This is my best dress. What's it called, where you're taking us?

KING: If I tell you, it won't be a surprise. (*He takes her hand, tenderly.*) And that's not the only surprise tonight.

SUSAN: What do you mean, dad?

KING: If I told you now, that'd be telling. It's a secret, wait 'til I tell you. You'll be so surprised, when you find out . . . over the liqueurs and cigars.

SUSAN: I don't have to smoke a cigar, do I?

KING: You make me laugh, Suzie. But I got enough cigars . . . every driver gave me a cigar this afternoon.

SUSAN: I couldn't be there, dad.

KING: I wish you had been.

SUSAN: I had to be at the hospital.

KING: You'd have been so proud of your old dad. I was quite overcome at the tributes my colleagues paid to me.

SUSAN: My duty . . . I couldn't change.

KING: It's not everyday that a father retires.

SUSAN: That's why I'm here tonight. I'd better put these in some water . . . they're for you. (*Now he takes the flowers.*)

KING: No-one has ever given me flowers. Not to me . . . How nice. Thank you Susan. What are these called?

SUSAN: They're irises.

KING: And these are called –

SUSAN: Gypsophila –

KING (*privately*): Sometimes they're called Baby's Breath . . . (*Turns to SUSAN.*) You've lost weight. (SUSAN *is arranging flowers in a vase now.*) You look skinny.

SUSAN: Do I?

KING: You're not eating properly.

SUSAN: I've been waiting for tonight.

KING: Nothing the matter? Because I worry about you when I don't see you. The doctors at the hospital behaving themselves, they not molesting you?

SUSAN: Dad!

KING: I've heard stories . . . patients waking up from the anaesthetic in the middle of their operation, seeing the surgeon molesting the nurses and taking off their clothes.

SUSAN: Don't believe all you hear dad.

KING: I care about you. Living in the nurses home. Ever since you left this house . . . I worry . . . what is the matter? You look so sad.

SUSAN: I am a bit sad.

KING: Tell your old dad. –

SUSAN: I'm a bit sad because . . . and this is the reason I didn't get away from the hospital this afternoon . . . you see . . . one of my patients . . . a really lovely woman . . . and I did the stupid thing, I cared about her too much, got personal, just like we're not supposed to . . . well, she's dying . . . it's very near . . . she might die tonight. The same illness as mum.

KING: I've been thinking a lot about Malley today. My guidance to you Susan, in times of distress . . . remember what you learned at Bible Class.

SUSAN: Yes dad.

KING: You know why I always used to come collect you and Linda? So I could wait outside and hear all you kiddies singing. I always liked that.

SUSAN: I always remember you waiting outside, when we came out. (*Pause.*)

KING: Mister Cunningham was talking about you this afternoon. He said, even as a child, your temperament impressed him so much, he'd marked you out to one day become his personal assistant. A secretary with your name on the door. (*They both laugh.*) He always knew, your heart was set on being a nurse.

SUSAN: That's right – though I'll be lucky if I'll be able to stay one much longer.

KING: Eh?

SUSAN: I mean, the way that caring Thatcher's butchering the NHS, I'll be lucky to keep my job.

KING: Susan! That is the Prime Minister you're talking about. And I will not have her name slandered and besmirched under my own roof. And –

SUSAN: Sorry, dad, sorry.

KING: And I find such sentiments particularly astonishing coming from another woman.

SUSAN: I'm sorry dad, but it makes me angry –

KING: And you make me angry, talk

like that. When we're having a civilised social glass of sherry to celebrate my retirement. And I do not want to get angry tonight.

SUSAN: I said I'm sorry. I am sorry. Very sorry. I don't want you to get angry –

KING: But I'm going to get damned angry if your sister is not here soon. You know what the time is?

SUSAN: About –

KING: The time precisely is; (*He jabs at digital watch.*) 14.27 and 32 . . . 33 . . . seconds.

SUSAN: I thought it was about eight –

KING (*jabs at watch*): This is six function . . . this is the time in Japan . . . this watch tells the time in every zone . . . what the damned time in London? (*Takes other watch from pocket.*) Linda should be here by now, or we'll be late! It's ten past eight.

SUSAN: Linda is always late.

KING: She'll be late for even her own damn funeral. The amazing thing is how she manages to hold down such a responsible job. The florist she works for must have the patience of Job.

SUSAN *relieved that* KING *is cooling down lets him pour her another sherry.*

Her idea of time keeping never used to be tolerated (SUSAN *grins at familiar hobby horse.*) Punctuality, my girl, used to be taken for granted. The youngsters at the depot nowadays, if they turn up for work on time they expect a bonus payment. It's –

SUSAN: It's shocking.

KING: It's bloody shocking. England is going to rack and ruin. There's no excuse for it. I was never late, never late –.

SUSAN: I know, dad. You mentioned it once or twice –

KING: I was not even late –

SUSAN: The winter when –

KING: The winter when the buses were on strike.

SUSAN: You set off before dawn –

KING: I set off from the old flat in Forest Gate on foot, before dawn, in the pitch dark, freezing below zero and the snow up to my waist and even then –

SUSAN: You were never late.

KING: I was never late. Mister Cunningham, in his speech at the presentation this afternoon, he made a great point about my punctuality record. He said, although I was retiring today . . . my exemplory punctuality record would remain an enduring inspiration.

SUSAN: His very words?

KING: Words to that effect. – It'll all be written up in the magazine. – And they took photographs of me with Mister Cunningham and the man who used to be a councillor on the GLC. It'll be in the magazine . . .

SUSAN (*holds his arm to inspect watch*): I'll order some. It lights up . . .

KING: Ah, so it does . . . very handy for seeing the time in the dark . . . six functions . . . but – (*Very close to* SUSAN *now. Hand in hand, face to face.*) But to give a man with a hundred per cent punctuality record an alarm watch . . .

SUSAN: It's the thought that counts.

KING: That's what I mean.

SUSAN: Is Linda bringing her boyfriend tonight?

KING: Have you met him?

SUSAN: No. Have you?

KING: No. And I don't like the sound of him.

SUSAN: Why not?

KING: Instinct. A very strong instinct. Linda told me where she met him.

SUSAN: Where?

KING: At the Dorchester Hotel. (*This triumphantly.* SUSAN *looks blank.*)

SUSAN: I don't get it.

KING: The Dorchester Hotel!

SUSAN: Yeah, sure – that's where Linda works, the florist shop at the –

KING: But what was *he* doing at the

Dorchester Hotel? Hmm? Why was he there when he's got a residence of his own in Tooting! A bit bloody suspicious, don't you think?

SUSAN: Oh, dad. I think it's best to keep an open mind. Since you haven't even met him yet!

KING: Indeed, I may not have met him. But I *have* seen his car. A Jaguar car. Linda drove it up here one day. I didn't like the look of its tyres.

SUSAN: Tyres?

KING: A very flashy Jaguar car, and the outside of the tyres are painted white. Bit flashy don't you think? For a Jaguar car. It look like it was balancing on a set of Polo mints! That a daughter of mine should . . . But I keep an open mind tonight. Even though I have grave misgivings about this chap. This man Linda is bringing to our *intimate* family occasion. I have told her of my doubts. But she just rattles her ear-rings down the telephone and ignores me.

SUSAN: Dad, I ought to get changed . . . put on my party dress . . . for the 'occasion'.

She kisses his cheek. Takes bag and goes. He holds the flowers. Stage darkens, just spotlight on him.

KING: They call these flowers . . . Baby's Breath. They were the flowers in your bouquet the day we got married, Malley. The preacher said: 'Will you take Malvina, Malvina.' He said: 'Wilt thou have this woman to thy wedded wife, to live together after God's ordinance in the Holy Estate of matrimony? Wilt thou love her, comfort her, honour and keep her in sickness and in health; and forsaking all other, keep thee only unto her, so long as ye both shall live?' (*Pause. Looks at flowers, also photo.*) I said . . . I will.

Banging on door. Lights up on room. The glow of the fire. KING places photo on trunk as SUSAN hurries in – nice dress, hair different.

SUSAN: The door dad, the door – didn't you hear it? Must be Linda. (KING confused, recovering from his

memories. SUSAN *pats his shoulder.*) I'll get it . . .

KING: Thank you.

SUSAN *has opened the door – ushers* LINDA *in. She's dressed like Diana Ross at Las Vegas.*

LINDA: Wow, daddy. What a suit! (*She passes* SUSAN *and waves arms at* KING's *buttoning jacket and tightening tie, respectfully.*) That is a sharp suit, daddy. You look sensational.

SUSAN: Hello, Linda.

LINDA: Dressed with such style! Hey man, you look like an admiral of the fleet and the Duke of Edinburgh and Darth Vader! Daddy, you look so dressed up, I feel like I'm not dressed up at all. (*Pause.* SUSAN *and* KING *exchange a glance.*)

KING: Linda, you are late.

LINDA: What a welcome!

KING: It is quarter past eight and we agreed –

LINDA: (*Laughing.*) Kissy, kissy, daddy . . . Ooooo . . . this smell you're wearing daddy, what is all this? What lady bought you this raunchy cologne? I mean – you smell like some horny wild man, daddy. What is this scene you're into: we are sisters and we should be told. (*She clasps* SUSAN *with conspiratorial arm.*)

KING: I'm telling you . . . you are late.

LINDA: Shit. (*Looks at* SUSAN.) What did he say to you, sister?

SUSAN: I was early.

LINDA: Typical. That's a lovely dress, Susan. Lovely colour, suits your personality, you should always wear grey. (*She goes to table for sherry glasses and bottle.*) Is this a buffet – shall I serve myself?

KING: Let me. (*He pours her a sherry.*) I thought you were coming with that Jaguar driver, thingy-me . . . what do you call him?

SUSAN: Stevie.

LINDA: Thank you, Susan.

KING: I thought Stephen –

LINDA: Stevie! Stevie has just gone to fill up with petrol. So we don't run out. He won't be two minutes, daddy. And he's so excited about tonight. Like I am. You made it sound so exciting – where we going? (*She has 'seduced'* KING. *Kisses him. He becomes coy.*)

KING: I tell you where we're going. We're going to just about the best damned restaurant in London.

SUSAN: Dad's arranged it all –

KING: I'm telling Linda, Susan.

SUSAN: I was just saying what you had –

KING: I'm quite capable to telling her myself. I may be 65 but I'm not demented.

SUSAN: I was just trying to –

LINDA: She was just trying to –

KING: I know what she meant. What I meant was: I thought this boyfriend of yours could have taken the precaution of getting sufficient petrol beforehand. Considering where we're going tonight.

LINDA: Tell him, Susan.

SUSAN: You haven't *said* where we're going tonight.

LINDA: Thank you, Susan. Not to mention – he's had a very busy day, daddy.

KING: A busy day doing what, exactly?

LINDA: Stevie owns three bingo shops. And today he has been negotiating the lease of shop number four.

KING: Bingo shops? You know my views on gambling.

SUSAN: Oh Dad, please –

LINDA: Daddy, I think you and Stevie are really going to get on like a house on fire. I just know you're going to like each other.

KING: I hope this is so. But –

LINDA: The only 'but' is – you've never ever liked any of my boyfriends. But Stevie is different . . . so please don't treat him like you treated all my other boyfriends and Susan's. This time, there's nothing to worry about. (*She's turned on party mood, roping in*

SUSAN. KING *laughs. They pour more sherry.*)

KING: With you and boyfriends, Linda – I always worried!

LINDA: Please, daddy. Don't remind me. How many embarrassments? How many times I nearly died? All those times . . . all those excuses you used to find to come downstairs in the middle of the night when I was entertaining . . . (*During following,* LINDA *and* SUSAN *act out these anecdotes, with fun.*)

KING: Entertaining? Is that what you called it?

LINDA (*mimicking* KING): 'I just come down here to make sure you got the fire on Linda and you're not gonna catch a cold.' And . . . 'Pardon me interrupting you Linda, but I just comed down from my bed because I think maybe I left the Bible down here . . . ah, here it is, under the cushions end of the sofa and your boyfriend's got his feet on it.' (LINDA *and* SUSAN *fall about laughing.* KING *enjoys this 'family warmth' as he'd describe it.*)

SUSAN: My worst moment was dad coming out to check the paint in the porch, whether it had dried . . . one o'clock in the morning on the doorstep –

LINDA: Andy Phelps!

SUSAN: Andy Phelps! 'Just you be careful with your clothes here, boy –'

LINDA: 'The paint might be a touch tacky – I only painted the porch last week'. (LINDA *and* SUSAN *hug each other, laughing.* KING *laughs heartily and downs another full glass of sherry.*)

KING: Trying to keep you two girls on the straight and narrow. (*They laugh more.*) If you'd been boys, known what to do. But two girls! Too much for one man alone.

SUSAN: I don't know how you managed on your own dad. I mean that seriously.

KING: And I seriously don't know how I never ended up a damned alcoholic!

SUSAN: But that's because Linda drank whatever you had in the cupboard!

KING: Eh?

LINDA (*accusing* SUSAN): You were in it with me. I couldn't have done it on me own, without you helping me. (*They start to demonstrate with drawers of sideboard – the drinks cupboard below the drawers.*)

KING: What I could never understand was how the level of the sherry bottles kept going down when I marked the bottle and locked the door and hid the key. So how . . . (LINDA *and* SUSAN *giggle and look at* KING *then at each other.*)

LINDA: Shall we show him?

SUSAN: Since he's going back to Trinidad on Wednesday, why not? (*The demonstration now in earnest.*)

LINDA: This is the door you locked, daddy. And hid the key. But above the locked door, this drawer. We just pulled it out, and reached in, pulled out the bottle . . . drank some, and put it back down . . . then put back the drawer. (*They all laugh.* LINDA *hugs* KING.) Well, now you know the whole truth.

KING: What I don't know, I'd rather never be told.

LINDA: I'm so excited about tonight, daddy. Please like Stevie . . . it's got to be a great night, it's not every night we're all together . . . the whole family. (*She kisses* KING, *notices* SUSAN *moodily mooching away.*)

LINDA: What's the matter with her? Is she all right?

KING: Your sister had an upsetting day at the hospital.

LINDA: She's too sensitive . . . for her own good.

KING: Exactly.

LINDA: Stevie's so excited about meeting you, he's going crazy to meet you, daddy. I've told him so much about you. He just loves it when I tell him funny stories about you. He says you've just got to be the greatest.

KING: Then I hope I don't disappoint him. If I fail to come on like the greatest, just kick my ankle and I'll try harder.

LINDA: Oh, daddy – you're so funny I could eat you.

During his embrace from LINDA, KING *has stared at* SUSAN, *feeling awkward, loitering by the front door. Horns on car sound outside. A more elaborate Colonel Bogey car horn sound. Then banging on front door.* SUSAN *opens it – revealing* STEVIE *dressed in sharp white suit, trilby hat and two-tone shoes.*

LINDA: That'll be Stevie . . . at last daddy . . . you're going to meet Stevie . . . this is my Stevie. (LINDA *has beckoned* STEVIE *in, by-passing* SUSAN *who had opened the door.*)

KING: Good evening. I am Linda's father.

STEVIE: Hi. Nice to meet you. In your house. Linda has told me so much about you.

KING: So I understand. My other daughter –

LINDA: This is my sister, Susan.

STEVIE: Hi.

SUSAN: 'Hi'.

LINDA: Hi hi hi. (*Pause.*)

SUSAN: I like your car.

STEVIE: Thanks.

SUSAN: I'll just finish getting changed. (*She goes.*)

LINDA: It's a great car. It's got electric windows and quadrophonic sound – you can sit in the front with Stevie, daddy. White leather seats. You'll just flip at the sound.

STEVIE: Better leg room, in the front, Mister King . . . (*He glances at the framed photo of* MALLEY.) That sure is a lady.

KING: My wife . . . Susan and Linda's mother.

STEVIE: I heard about her.

KING: She's dead.

STEVIE: I heard such nice things about her. (KING *replaces photo as*

STEVIE *paces, taking in room.*) Nice house. It feels . . . homely. I don't know about families . . . but this feels like a homely, family house. (*Pause.*)

KING: I understand you live in Tooting. (*Pause.*)

STEVIE: That's right. I have a place in Tooting. Where exactly are we going, Mister King?

KING: Dean Street. A restaurant in Dean Street. Do you know where Dean Street is?

STEVIE: Sure, sure I do. I know it well enough.

KING: It's in Soho.

STEVIE: Then we're talking about the same Dean Street.

KING: I have reserved a table at a restaurant there for nine o'clock. The traffic on a Friday night –

STEVIE: We've got plenty of time.

KING: To park a car in Soho on a Friday night –

STEVIE: I know a place.

KING: I think we best be on our way now.

STEVIE: I agree. I think everything's under control. I think it's cool, we're doing just fine. As long as – like you say Mister King – we start on our way right now. Let's go . . . (*He walks out. LINDA hugs KING. Sound of car starting outside.*)

LINDA: I just knew you and Steve would get on like a house on fire, daddy. You must sit in the front with Stevie. He'll show you how to operate the electric windows and the sound system. Oh, daddy! For one terrible minute I thought you were going to wear this stupid thing! (*She removes his scarf and hurries out, laughing. KING drains glass of sherry. SUSAN has come in and is watching him. Revs of car engine outside and 'sound system'.*)

SUSAN: You ok, dad?

KING: Sure, sure.

SUSAN: Are you sure you're ok?

KING: I've met friendlier men.

SUSAN: He's probably very nervous about meeting you. I thought he was trying very hard to be friendly. And respectful. Come on – the Polo mint chariot awaits us. (*Stage goes to black, just a spotlight on KING as he puts on his raincoat.*)

KING: Malley, I really do wish you was going to be there in the restaurant tonight.

I feel so strange and nervous. Like I felt when I set sail . . . I can still see you there on the wharf, Malley – waving me goodbye. The sun shining. You in a flowered dress, blowing me kisses till the distance took you away from me. It was such a long wait 'til I could send you the ticket to come. Then the joy of your coming. So lovely, Malley, you and me together. Then Linda was born. And then Susan. Two beautiful daughters. And now, tonight – Tonight, Malley . . . in the restaurant when I tell the girls our surprise. I think you would agree it's the right thing to do, had you been here. (*Changing watches.*) I'll take this off . . . and wear the watch you gave me. Because tonight is our night, Malley. Mine and yours. All we worked for – and the things we achieved together . . . For Susan and Linda.

I think you'll agree I done the right thing, Malley. I *feel* sure . . . you'll agree.

Scene Two

The restaurant in Soho.

A corner table. KING *sits at it with* LINDA, STEVIE *and* SUSAN *as they study menus the size of broadsheet newspapers.* WAITER *arrives with tray of drinks.*

WAITER: Excuse me, monsieur. Your aperitifs.

KING: Ah yes, our drinks. I was just starting to wonder what had happened to the aperitifs I'd ordered for us.

WAITER: For madame. And I believe, for the other madame –

STEVIE: And this looks like mine.

(Takes it.)

WAITER: The whiskey sour, monsieur . . . and the Pernod is for –

KING: That is for me. That's what I ordered. *(He takes it.)*

WAITER: Le Pernod, monsieur. Trés bon. Water monsieur? *(Pouring it.)*

KING: I always find that Pernod is the most agreeable aperitif before cordon bleu cuisine. Don't you agree?

WAITER: Monsieur is a gourmet.

KING: Quite, quite.

LINDA: Daddy, please. Don't embarrass us. *(She and SUSAN keep glancing around behind plants to other diners.)*

KING *(to WAITER)*: Take no notice of my daughter. These are daughters. This is a rather extra-special occasion, me bringing them here for dinner tonight on account of the celebration –

SUSAN: Dad, now you're embarrassing me!

KING: I'm entertaining my family tonight, no expense spared. When I say my family, Stevie – with all due respect . . .

STEVIE: I understand, Mister King. I hear you.

KING: The occasion is to celebrate my retirement.

WAITER: Monsieur does not look old enough.

KING: I beg your pardon?

WAITER: Monsieur does not look old enough.

KING: I am 65. I can prove it –

SUSAN: Dad, for Christ's sake! He's only –

LINDA: I think he got the message daddy, when we came in and you told him the first time and ordered the aperitifs . . .

STEVIE: I got an idea he got the message, Mister King.

KING: All I'm saying is: it's not every day a man retires . . .

WAITER: Le patron asks that, please,

you will accept the aperitifs on the house . . . to celebrate the occasion.

KING: That is most civilised. When you say Le Patron, I presume you mean the manager of the restaurant?

WAITER: Oui, monsieur.

SUSAN: Who the hell do you think he means dad – the busker in the alleyway outside?

KING: Then tell Le Patron I consider his offer most agreeable and I'd consider it an honour if he'd care to have a drink on me. Just add it to my bill.

LINDA: Oh shit.

WAITER: You are too kind. Are you ready to order, monsieur?

KING: We haven't quite finished reading the menu yet.

WAITER: Then I will return when you have –

KING *grabs his sleeve, preventing* WAITER *going away.*

KING: Psst! Tell me, man, is there anything that you particularly recommend here?

WAITER: Everything is excellent here, monsieur – as I am sure you know.

KING: To tell you the truth –

SUSAN: Dad!

KING: To tell you the truth, as a matter of fact –

LINDA: You don't have to tell him your life story, daddy.

KING: As a matter of fact, to tell you the truth this is the first time I've been here. To dine. But I have received the highest recommendation for this restaurant from Mister Cunningham. *(Pause.)*

WAITER: Ah, Monsieur Cunningham, of course.

KING: Quite. Monsieur Cunningham was a senior colleague of mine at the Stratford depot. In fact he presented my retirement present to me today. Mister Cunningham spoke highly of this restaurant when he dined here to celebrate his silver wedding. Which is why I chose it tonight. (STEVIE *starts to order, to cover the excruciating embarrassment.)*

STEVIE: Le soupe quatre champignons de la forêt à mousse à l'orange –

WAITER: Sir, that is a soup of four different flavours of mushrooms with – (*The digital alarm starts playing Yellow Rose of Texas.*)

KING: What is it? This stupid music?

STEVIE: It sounds like a digital watch alarm.

SUSAN: It's your watch, dad. God. Switch it off – everyone's looking at us.

KING: Quite right. It's the alarm.

LINDA: Switch the damn thing off, dad.

KING: Easier said than done, Linda. I haven't the instructions with me. There's six functions . . . and only three buttons. Ah! That's the illuminating light, most convenient for seeing the digits in the dark. (*This to* WAITER.)

LINDA: Just switch it off, daddy.

SUSAN: Press all of them, dad – press *these*!

She leans across table to press them. In doing so knocks KING's *Pernod into his lap. He leaps up.*

KING: God, Christ. Look what you've done.

LINDA: At least it's stopped the alarm.

SUSAN: Sorry, dad. I didn't mean it to splash over your trousers.

KING: Here, monsieur – I wipe for you before it makes the stain.

KING *outraged at* WAITER *wiping his personal parts. Takes napkin.*

KING: Take your hands off me! Thanks all the same, but I'll do that.

WAITER: As monsieur pleases. I shall bring you another Pernod – then perhaps you are ready to order your meal.

WAITER *goes.* KING *dries trousers.*

SUSAN: I'm so sorry, dad.

KING: Nothing to worry about, nothing to worry about. Now let's concentrate on the important thing: What are we going to eat?

LINDA: What's this, Stevie?

STEVIE: Fillets de Maquereau à la dieppoise – poached mackerel in white wine sauce.

KING: You speak French very well, Stevie.

SUSAN: You should know, dad.

STEVIE: Thank you, Mister King.

LINDA: Stevie's uncle is a French chef.

STEVIE (*to* KING): That's what my uncle calls himself. I don't actually think he's a chef at all – I reckon he's just a kitchen hand.

SUSAN: Where?

STEVIE: The Dorchester Hotel.

KING: The Dorchester Hotel? (*Looks at* SUSAN.) I *see.*

LINDA: So I'll start with the mackerel and then for the main course . . . the steak au poivre.

KING: *As a matter* of fact, Linda . . . I was just thinking of the mackerel myself . . . (*The alarm Yellow Rose of Texas has started again.*) Good God. Why has it started alarming again?

STEVIE: I think, Mister King, you pressed for snooze instead of stopping –

KING: It's only got three damned buttons to press!

STEVIE: I believe it's the combination in which you press them for the six functions –

SUSAN: Why have you got that watch in your pocket – I mean, why aren't you wearing it?

KING: Don't be so damned stupid, Susan. I didn't think it was going to start setting off the alarm at nine o'clock at night – it's supposed to start alarm calls at nine o'clock in the morning.

LINDA: Can't you just stop the noise, daddy?

KING: How?

STEVIE: I think you need a pin to re-set the time signals, Mister King.

LINDA: Just switch it all off, please.

KING: I haven't had sufficient time to study and fully digest all the instructions yet, Linda.

STEVIE: Mr King, use a fork – prod at the buttons – like this. (STEVIE *does so. Alarm stops.*)

KING: Thank you very much, Stevie. Now, what did we say we are all having for first course?

SUSAN: I'll have the chicken mousse.

KING: It sounds very palatable.

SUSAN: So I'll have that.

STEVIE: And I'd like to have the chef's paté, if you approve Mister King.

LINDA: And I'll have the mackerel.

KING: That's what I thought I'd have, Linda.

LINDA: Ok – let's have the mackerel special twice.

WAITER *arrives, gives* KING *fresh Pernod and prepares to take orders.*

WAITER: You are ready to order now?

KING: Almost, almost. It seems a waste if we both have the same thing. Why don't you have something different as a starter, and I'll have the mackerel.

LINDA: Ok, Ok. Let's do that then.

WAITER: One mackerel.

SUSAN: Chicken mousse.

LINDA: Escargots for me.

KING: An excellent choice Linda.

STEVIE: And the chef's paté, please.

WAITER: And for your main course?

KING: For me, the Beouf Wellington.

WAITER: That is for two persons monsieur.

KING: Precisely. Stevie, I thought you'd join me with that? It's most succulent. Mister Cunningham had it when he was here and he recommended it very highly.

STEVIE: I'd love to, Mister King.

LINDA: The steak au poivre, rare.

SUSAN: And I'll have the dover sole, please. Just plain.

WAITER: Grilled?

SUSAN: Grilled. No fancy stuff.

KING: But are you sure, Susan? There's so many sauces and concoctions you could have. You can select any way you want it cooked –

SUSAN: Just plain. Thank you.

KING: Well, I must say, it seems like a damned waste to me, quite frankly. Coming all the way to Soho, to a restaurant renowned for its cuisine . . . which is . . . (*To* WAITER.) It is true to say, is it not, that this restaurant is almost world famous?

WAITER: Perhaps, monsieur. In Dean Street. (*Everyone laughs.*) I will bring a selection of vegetables.

KING: Psst! And also, while you're in the kitchen . . . if you could find and bring back some sort of little pin, to fix the watch, to re-set the alarm.

WAITER: A pin monsieur. To re-set your alarm.

KING: I'm just anxious that The Yellow Rose of Texas doesn't keep playing every five minutes.

STEVIE: I'm sure he feels the same way, Mister King. (*To* WAITER.) We'd like the wine list –

KING: Ah yes, the wine list. (*Snatching it en route to* STEVIE.) Now let me see . . .

LINDA: Actually, daddy, tonight Stevie would like to.

STEVIE: If this doesn't offend you, Mister King . . . with my business, I've had a very lucky day so –

LINDA: It looks like the new shop's going through so –

SUSAN: That's wonderful news. Excuse me.

STEVIE: It'd be nice if you'd let me buy the wine.

KING: Champagne!!! You get the first bottle and I'll get the next one . . . now what have we here . . . (*He looks at wine list.*)

STEVIE: Garcon (*To* WAITER.) a bottle of Dom Perignon. Very cold.

KING: Yes, and bring it here in a bucket of ice. To make sure it's extremely cold . . . if that's not putting you to no

inconvenience. (WAITER *goes.*
KING's *eyes hit wine list.*) Dom
Perignon. God Christ . . . The price!

STEVIE: I buy the second bottle Mister
King, both bottles tonight. Please.

LINDA: Stevie's fourth shop has gone
through and when the luck's in –

STEVIE & LINDA: When the luck's in –
you might as well enjoy it. (*They both
laugh at their private joke. They hug.*)

LINDA: Stevie says I'm his lucky
mascot.

STEVIE: Ever since I met her, my luck
has changed. What are you thinking,
Mister King?

KING: I was thinking about champagne
. . . I'm starting to acquire the taste
. . . though I never drunk champagne
before today . . . there was enough
though this afternoon at the canteen to
bath in . . . so much champagne . . .
you know, I could have a shower in it.

WAITER *arrives with bottle and ice
bucket behind* KING; KING *sips
Pernod, oblivious to* WAITER *behind
him.*

My old Uncle Albert, I was just
thinking what he used to say.

He wouldn't even touch wine. He had
such a biasedness concerning French
people. It went back to . . . well, what
he used to tell me was: How can you
trust the Frogs? When they're jumping
up and down in the barrel to crush the
grapes, how can you be sure they
won't have a pee pee in the grape
juice.

KING *horrified to see* WAITER
beside him, hearing this 'racist' joke.
WAITER *doesn't open the
champagne bottle.* SUSAN, LINDA
and STEVIE *laugh.*

Oh my God!

KING *approaches us in spotlight.
Stage goes to dark to enable table to
be re-set – for after the meal.*

Oh my God . . . if only you were here
with me tonight Malley, I would not
behave so stupidly. I wouldn't be so
jumpy. (*Wipes his face with
handkerchief.*) Such a meal. How they
can charge such prices, I . . . but never

mind. Malley . . . hold my hand,
darling . . . (*Flexes hand.*) Feel your
hand in mine . . . now . . . because
now I will tell our daughters . . . the
surprise.

Lights up on restaurant table.
WAITER *has poured brandies, set
coffee cups and is lighting* KING's
cigar as he returns to table. STEVIE
has LINDA *light his smaller cigar.
Brandy bottle left on table.*

WAITER: Anything else, monsieur?

KING: Thank you, no.

WAITER: As monsieur pleases.

KING: Monsieur will be pleased to not
be interrupted. (WAITER *bows and
goes.*)

STEVIE: Wonderful meal, Mister King.

KING: Thank you. I have something to
tell my daughters.

LINDA: Speech, speech.

KING: I'm not a great speech maker.

LINDA: Speech.

KING: All right, Linda, all right. I say, I
know I'm not a speech maker but . . .
I have something special to say
tonight, tonight here in London, the
night I have retired.

LINDA: Congratulations, daddy – you
don't look old enough –

KING: Please, shut your mouth Linda.
Wha'ppen, girl, you drunk?

LINDA: Daddy!

STEVIE: Linda, your father was
saying –

KING: Thank you. I have something
important to tell you. When I arrived
in England, nearly forty years ago . . .
I didn't think things could have turned
out so well. Next week, on Wednesday
I will return to the island that I came
from.

LINDA: Trinidad!

KING: I'm not raising this glass to toast
where I came from –

LINDA: Trinidad!

KING: Nor where I'm going to. I want
to toast where I have been, all these
years. Since when I stepped off that

boat in Southampton, the cold, windy February morning – that lifetime ago. I find it very hard . . . to explain . . . I feel very emotioned. (*Pause.*)

SUSAN: Go on, dad. We're listening.

KING: Words to express these emotions . . . when I stepped off that vessel . . . wearing a suit too inadequate for the cold and a pair of shoes that mashed my feet, with so many others, making this journey from our islands. Comed here at the invitation of . . . no, damn it, we came at the begging request of England after the war. The mother country. When we came ashore, all of us . . . we expected Mister Churchill to be waiting on the quayside with his big fat cigar . . . to welcome us. He was not there. Then losing sight of the friends I'd made on the boat in the chaos at Waterloo Station . . . our belongings in our cases, just dumped in the middle of the platform while we waited for the British Council. Some cases were stolen – we saw spivs pick them up and walk away with them. We thought they were station porters. At first, when they showed the room in Forest Gate . . . so cold, with the whole house smelling of disinfectant . . . we wondered, the friends I'd made on the voyage . . . we wondered . . . was this such a good welcome we had expected? Missed the sunshine, and the noise and the smells back home. And I missed your mother. It wasn't the green fields and Government house voices and Buckingham Palace. Not the room in Forest Gate. It was an inauspicious beginning.

But! I made it! I made a life here in England, a life beyond dreams. I joined London Transport. I swept platforms, for two years. I made friends with the drivers. I drank tea with them in the canteen. Learned the tricks of their trade. The requirements. I took their advice. There was a great shortage after the war of reliable, responsible men. My attitude impressed. I never caused no trouble. I was always punctual and dependable.

I got the training as a driver, because I had proved my worth. I got a mortgage. The house. And then I sent for your mother . . . to come here and join me, and make a family and a life here in England. And a very good life indeed. Beyond my wildest dreams. Never short of food, decent clothes, excellent schools, holidays, a television . . . a comfortable home. And two daughters of whom I am so very, very proud. If Malley was here tonight she would say exactly that. If she had not died, then I think we would have stayed here after I retired . . . I really am so proud of you girls . . . Susan . . . (*Clinks her glass.*) our Florence Nightingale. (*They laugh.*) Even though if Mister Cunningham had had his way, you could have been his personal private assistant with your name on the door. (*They all laugh at this old family joke.*) And Linda . . . with her artistic flair . . . and after a series of false starts –

LINDA: Oi, dad.

KING: A florist with the most reputable florist business in one of the grandest hotels in the world. And now, my surprise for tonight . . . (*He takes envelope from inside pocket of suit jacket and withdraws legal deeds which he spreads on table.*) The mortgage to the house is now all paid. Not a penny owed. I own it.

SUSAN: Really?

KING: See for yourself, daughter. Thirty year mortgage, the last instalment I paid last month. When Malley and I took on the mortgage, the value of the house was just less than one thousand pounds –

SUSAN: Now it must be worth . . . what? Forty-five thousand?

LINDA: More!

KING: Exactly . . . On Wednesday I am going back to Trinidad; I am going to live with your Auntie Rose and Uncle James. So I don't need the house. That is why I got a solicitor to change the deeds of ownership of the house . . .

SUSAN: Deeds of ownership –

LINDA: I don't know what you mean, daddy. (*She looks at* STEVIE.)

STEVIE: Seems Linda thinks, because I have to deal a lot with lawyers in my business . . . she seems to think I know what you're talking about, but I don't. I never heard about deeds of ownership unless you mean –

KING: What I mean, is this is a change of ownership contract. Here I give my house to my daughters – one half to Susan, one half to Linda. It is your house now. Well, what do you say?

SUSAN: I'm a bit speechless, dad . . . I don't know what to say. What are you saying . . . what do you mean? You want to give me and Linda *your* house?

KING: I never thought of it as my house. I always thought of it as the family home . . . I own it. But now I'm not going to live in it anymore I want to transfer the ownership to you and Linda. What do you say, Linda?

LINDA: I just can't believe it, I really cannot believe what you're saying, daddy. (STEVIE *has been studying the contract on the table.*)

STEVIE: What he's saying is what he's got his solicitor to do on this contract here. If you sign it, you become the owners of the house.

KING: All you have to do is sign, on the dotted line.

STEVIE: There and there.

STEVIE *is very suspicious.* KING *avoids* STEVIE's *searching stares.*

SUSAN: Now wait a minute, dad. This is crazy. You spent all your working life to buy that house . . . and now you're retired, and you've got to live on a pension and –

KING: And my savings. I've got my pension and my savings.

LINDA: And, of course, Auntie Rose probably won't charge you any rent when you get back to Trinidad. (*She tries to laugh it off.*) Of course, I didn't really mean that . . . I don't know what to say . . .

KING: No, no, no – you're right Linda. Auntie Rose won't charge me a damned penny rent.

SUSAN: But, dad, the point is . . . you worked for thirty five years to buy the house. Now if it's paid for . . .

STEVIE (*to* SUSAN *having carefully checked deed*): It's paid for, sure.

SUSAN: Then you should reap the benefits. Sell it, make a bomb.

KING: I don't want to sell it. I want to give it to my daughters.

SUSAN: You could make so much money out of it.

KING: I don't want to make money. I make sixty thousand pounds, it'd be like going back home a millionaire. Auntie Rose would never let me live in her house if I –

SUSAN: OK, OK, if you don't want to sell it – rent the house. Then you've got an income . . . as well as your savings.

KING: Do I look like a landlord? Me? Susan, I would hate the idea of other people living in our family house. That's why I want you and Linda to have it, and enjoy it – my daughters reap the benefits of all I've worked for.

SUSAN: We could just live in it. Without owning it.

LINDA: But wait a minute, Susan. Daddy seems to have made up his mind.

SUSAN: It's too ridiculous for words, dad.

KING: I want my two wonderful, wonderful daughters to be the owners of the house. It will make me so wonderfully happy.

SUSAN: Sleep on it. This is such an emotional time.

KING: It is what I have always intended. I want you both to sign it now, tonight, here. Please.

LINDA: Well, I think this is the most amazing, kind and generous gift I've ever heard anyone giving. Oh daddy, you're such an incredible man. (*She kisses his cheek.*)

KING: I've been incredibly lucky. I came to this country with nothing . . . just the clothes I stood up in. So I'm the lucky one. Thanks to England, I can give to my daughters a house. I'm the one who's grateful. So I propose we all drink a toast to the mother country, a toast to England. (*He raises glass and stands.*) To England.

LINDA: To England.

STEVIE: To England. (*Silence. They all look at* SUSAN.)

KING: Susan, we are drinking a toast to England, the mother country. (*Pause. She doesn't look up.*)

SUSAN: Some bloody mother.

KING: I said, a toast to –

SUSAN: I'll drink a toast to you, dad. Willingly I'll drink to you and everything you have achieved.

KING: The toast I proposed is to England.

SUSAN: I can't. I'll drink to you dad but not to England.

LINDA: Don't be so difficult, you stupid bitch.

SUSAN: I'm not being difficult. I just don't feel especially grateful to England.

LINDA: Daddy is. For him –

SUSAN: Daddy might well feel grateful to England. But it's my country, I was born here so –

KING: But I wasn't. Then I came here and I made a helluva better life than if I'd –

SUSAN: That was thirty five years ago, dad. How long have you got to go on being grateful? The rest of your life? Not that England seems to hold lives too precious nowadays.

KING: What's got into you? What you preaching? This black power talk?

SUSAN: I'm talking about the way this country . . . *my* country . . . how a woman in my ward is dying tonight because England is too mean to spend money on –

KING: What, Lord God, has this got to do with what I'm saying?

LINDA: Susan, you're upsetting daddy.

STEVIE: Hey, why don't you both cool down a little.

KING: The way I see it –

SUSAN: You don't see it at all. You're not looking at the world as it really is. The England you're talking about is some fantasy!

KING: Fantasy! What the heavens – you stop being so personal.

SUSAN: It's a delusion. You're deceiving yourself.

LINDA: Susan, shut up.

STEVIE: Perhaps this isn't the time or place –

SUSAN: He asked me. The England I see is the one that ought to be grateful to black men like you who worked their arses off for –

KING: Now you leave my arse out of this, daughter. (*He hammers table.*)

STEVIE: Mister King, wouldn't it be a good idea to –

KING: You hold your tongue, boy.

LINDA: There's no need to shout! We're sitting right next to you – (WAITER *arrives as they all talk at once.*)

WAITER: Is everything to your satisfaction?

KING: Yes, Yes.

LINDA (*aside to* STEVIE): A commotion like this – they'll never let us in here again.

WAITER: If there is anything else you want . . . just . . . monsieur. (WAITER *goes.*)

SUSAN: I'm sorry dad. I didn't want to cause a row. I wasn't being personal. I can't stop thinking about a woman who . . . a *white* woman . . . who is slowly and cruelly dying inch by inch tonight . . .

KING: What has this got to do with me?

LINDA: This is boring.

SUSAN: I'll tell you what it's got to do with you dad. When mum died, that's when I absolutely knew for sure that I wanted to be a nurse. That was eleven years ago, right. Then it seemed that everything that was humanly possible was done for mum. But now, I don't feel that. All the scientific advances that have been made . . . and she will die tonight because the money that could be spent isn't. Hospitals are being closed. In my hospital we are 198 staff nurses short. I'm not saying she's been neglected. I'm not saying she wouldn't have died anyway. But they had closed the breast testing centre, so she never had the early warning. She had to wait to get radio therapy because there is such a chronic shortage of equipment. Radio therapy makes the skin burn – like acute sunburn. When her relatives asked for calamine lotion they were told to buy it themselves. Because of the budget cut back. The air conditioning was switched off in the summer, to save the cost of running it. She used to be exquisitely beautiful. She showed me photographs when she was young . . . now there's hardly anything of her. She weighs three and a half stone. The chemotherapy made her bald . . . and she'll die tonight. (SUSAN *wipes her eyes.*) I'll drink to you, dad. But I won't drink to this country. I'm sorry if it hurts you, but it's what I feel: this country, now, doesn't care about its weak, or its poor or its ill. Not really care. Because that costs money . . . it's cheaper to let people die. I will never drink a toast to England.

KING: You will toast England or I swear to God I will strike out your name on this contract.

SUSAN: Then I will not have half of the house.

KING: Such ingratitude!

SUSAN: How many times does anyone have to say thank you? And why are you giving us the house under these conditions anyway, you vain, vain, vain man!

KING (*bellows*): Get out of my sight, out of my sight. (SUSAN *hesitates. Then after glancing at LINDA, gathers her bag from under the table and hurries out. WAITER arrives with coffee.*)

STEVIE: Put it down, put it down and go. (STEVIE'*s authority ensures the* WAITER *does this.* KING *with his head in his hands now.*)

KING: Is she really going?

STEVIE: Yes, Mister King. Shall I go,

bring her back . . .? (LINDA *grabs* STEVIE'*s wrist, halting this notion.*)

LINDA: I don't think anyone could bring her back. She's made up her mind.

STEVIE: I'll try and find her (*He goes.*)

KING: She's gone?

LINDA: Yes, she's gone, daddy.

KING: Then she is not my daughter. She is an ungrateful bitch (LINDA *pushes* STEVIE *away and moves chair beside her weeping father to comfort him.*)

LINDA: Please, daddy – don't be too hard on her. She's obviously very upset about this patient of hers in the hospital tonight . . . but even so, there was no need for her to be so heartless . . . tonight of all nights . . . I know just how you feel daddy. Susan can be so cruel, the things she says. She's just not like you and me at all.

KING: Of the two of you, I always thought Susan . . . she was the . . .

LINDA: But you always treated us both the same, daddy. You never showed any favouritism . . . even with the house, you were going to give it to both of us . . . To me, as well as to Susan.

KING: The way Susan spoke to me . . . (*He flops his head on table,* LINDA *fiddles with his pen, which he had produced to sign deed.*)

LINDA: But daddy, if we had done all this . . . it would only have been in name.

KING: A legal document –

LINDA: But to me, it would have always been your house. Like it is now. So, OK – if it was 'legally' Susan and mine's . . . well, it would always have been there for you whenever you wanted to come back to it. And after you've gone to Trinidad I'm sure you will keep popping back . . . I hope . . . because the thought of not seeing you so often, upsets me so much . . . (*Now* KING *comforts her.*)

KING: There, there Linda . . . you're a good daughter. A good girl.

LINDA: In the past, daddy, sometimes I've been naughty . . . but –

KING: All girls are naughty sometimes, but in your heart –

LINDA: Oh, in my heart! Yes, always . . . and it breaks my heart, daddy, to think that because of Susan's ingratitude, other people, strangers will now live in that house of ours where we all used to be so happy . . .

KING: Oh, oh . . . ah . . . the house.

LINDA: I tell you what . . . if you don't have time before you go on Wednesday . . . to sort it all out, then I'll arrange for an estate agent who specialises in leasing to fix up the letting of it. And I'll ensure that the rent is sent to you every month at Auntie Rose's.

KING: The house, ah the house. It is done. It is the contract here . . . so . . . the solution is . . . I cross out Susan's name.

LINDA: Can you do that, daddy?

KING: Watch me, I am doing it. So! And if you and I sign . . . then the house will be all yours, yours alone.

LINDA: I'm not sure about this.

KING: It is my wish, Linda.

LINDA: It's so complicated, the legal side . . . I don't really know about these things . . . but I think you ought to initial each cancellation daddy . . . (*He does so.*)

KING: Now I want you to sign it.

LINDA: Are you really sure?

KING: Please, Linda.

LINDA: You can always change your mind.

KING: I will not change my mind. (LINDA *signs.*)

LINDA: I'll have to get a witness. (*She looks up.* STEVIE *is standing behind her. He has been there for a while, without her knowing.*) Stevie, will you –

STEVIE: Me?

LINDA: Daddy would like you to be the legal witness.

STEVIE: Your father . . . or *you* would like me to –

KING: Yes, please, Stevie . . . if you would . . . I will be most grateful . . . (STEVIE *takes pen offered by* LINDA *and signs. Sits.*)

STEVIE: You don't have to be grateful, Mister King.

LINDA: You have made me so happy, daddy – I think I might cry. (STEVIE *watches* LINDA *slide the signed deeds into her handbag.*)

KING: Tears of joy . . . My heart is broken. I am making a damned fool of myself . . . Why did she do this to me . . . did you find her, Stevie? (STEVIE *shakes his head. He's appalled at* KING's *grief.*) I must go out . . . get out . . . before I make a fool of myself in front of the whole damned restaurant . . . (*He staggers towards exit:* LINDA *makes token gesture.*)

LINDA: Please daddy, don't go – please don't. (STEVIE *begins to rise to actually prevent* KING *leaving.* LINDA *restrains* STEVIE. KING *has taken brandy bottle.*) I think he wants to be on his own for a little while . . . (STEVIE *sits, watching* LINDA. *She lights a cigarette.*) Poor old sod. What a disastrous evening it all turned out to be for him.

STEVIE: Apart from you . . .

LINDA: Eh?

STEVIE: I mean, apart from how nice you been to him . . . just now. (*She sips her drink and exhales smoke.*) Where is the mother fucking contract, Linda.

LINDA: In my mother fucking bag.

STEVIE: What's the game. You intend to keep it?

LINDA: He gave it to me.

STEVIE: Yes . . . yes . . . so he did. And you sure did that well.

LINDA: What do you mean?

STEVIE: I mean: the way you got him to sign it over to you.

LINDA: It's what he wanted.

STEVIE: When you told him to! Sister, you could charm the crap out of a deep fried fucking turtle.

LINDA: Don't be vulgar, it upsets me.
He wanted to get it over with.

STEVIE: The state that old guy's in!

LINDA: Because of the state he's in . . .
that's why I got him to sign it and give
it to me. The mad mood he's in
tonight, poor daddy. The state Susan
got him into. If he'd strolled off round
Soho with this in his pocket, he could
have got the first cider-methy tramp to
sign it, cross our names out and given
the house to a complete stranger.

STEVIE: Whoever he gave it away to
. . . it couldn't have been more
madder than giving it to you.

LINDA: We can do a lot with sixty five
grand Stevie.

STEVIE: Oh it's 'we' now is it?

LINDA: He can't take the house with
him back to Trinidad.

STEVIE: Give the old man some
respect. How long you think he's
gonna stay there?

LINDA: Forever.

STEVIE: Come on. I can understand
him going back. Maybe he'll stay for a
few months. But his world is here, in
London. And you and your sister are
his world. Now he's retired from his
job . . . it's all he's got.

LINDA: I don't know about that –

STEVIE: It might not be much. But I
can't see what else he's got. Where do
you think he might have gone?

LINDA: Probably taking the tube home.
Sitting in the driving cab on the
Central Line, telling the driver about
his 'exemplary punctuality record.'
He's been drinking a lot . . .

STEVIE: Yeah?

LINDA: Champagne all day, sherry at
the house and tonight he's taken the
bottle. Don't look at me like that
Stevie, Christ, you must have seen how
vain he is.

STEVIE: Sure, sure. I seen a lot of
things tonight. (WAITER *arrives with
bill.* LINDA *laughs.*)

LINDA: The distinguished gentleman
who invited us here tonight –

STEVIE: Linda –

LINDA: He's done a runner, my son.
Without paying the bleeding bill.

WAITER: Madame?

LINDA: Say it again. I just love your
French accent – whereabouts in
Hackney do you come from?

STEVIE: I pay with plastic – you take
American Express.

WAITER: Thank you, monsieur.

STEVIE: Fast. Make it fast . . . there's
an old man out there tonight I've got
to find . . . after I've taken you home
darling, to your sixty five grand house.
(*Holds her face.* WAITER *has gone.*)
Then I go look for Mister King . . .
wherever he is tonight.

Music: Marley's 'No Woman No Cry'.

ACT TWO

Scene One

Music: Marley's Time Will Tell.

Stratford Shunting Yard. Wild open space and spotlights on towers. Tannoy announcement of last train to Shoeburyness. Sound of train departing and then we see KING staggering drunkenly as trains pass – he's dishevelled and carries brandy bottle from the restaurant.

KING: (*shouts to signal box*): Hey, you up there. Can you hear me. Yes, you. You in your computerised signalbox. Press a damned button and divert every Inter City train to Southend and off the end of the pier . . . into the blasted sea. Demolish Canvey Island.

This is *me*. Thomas Gilbert King. I am a man standing here. See me . . . in the light. Not all steel round about, and shunting metal tracks and clanging trains . . . I am a man . . . with human emotions . . . with a beatin' heart and a bleeding soul . . . I am a man. Dying of heartbreak . . . can you see him? It is me!

Spotlight beams pick him out in a mist of dazzling blinding white light as he staggers, tripping over a train line. He has carefully, like a drunk is careful, stepped over several elaborately until this trip. A train screams past from stage left to right, the noise and wind very fast. Shuddering shadows over fallen KING. When it has passed.

Fifteen million tins of Heinz baked beans shooting through the night to Welwyn Garden City. Enough baked beans to fart the roof off the town hall of Welwyn Garden City.

Another express cargo train passes from right to left just as KING manages to stand – causing him to fall again. When it has gone.

Trans continental containers . . . a billion tons of Polish coal fast bound to Cardiff and Swansea . . . diesel trains . . . electric trains . . . I want to drown in vapours of coal boiled steam . . . Can you see me, you can kill me! (*This another shout to signal box.*) Swish the computer levers re-set the track . . .

and you can send the Polish coal back to Poland or fifteen million tons of baked beans to Cardiff instead of Polish coal . . . or press my pants like tissue paper in the rain . . . with me in them . . . I am crying . . . I am crying . . . I can rust the rails . . . rot the old oak sleepers with my drizzling tears. I am an old man . . . crying here . . . for thirty five years this station was my depot . . . and now I don't know where I am . . .

He staggers, swigs from brandy bottle. Torchlight beam and voice, Scottish accent, from behind him. Enter JIMMY.

JIMMY: Hey . . . you there. You seen my whippet?

KING: Pardon me?

JIMMY: I said – you don't happen to have my whippet there with you?

KING: What sort of whippet?

JIMMY: What are you inquiring after? The pedigree?

KING: I haven't seen no whippet.

JIMMY: You look like a man I can trust. (*Shines torch beam in his face.*)

KING: I haven't seen any dog.

JIMMY: Not any? That's beyond belief . . . this is exactly the sort of night dogs run wild here.

KING: Here?

JIMMY: Mostly, they're dead time I find them.

KING: Dead dogs?

JIMMY: You'd be surprised . . . how many dead dogs you can find here some nights.

KING: What sort of nights?

JIMMY: After Christmas, they're the worst nights. You mind if I have a drop.

KING: Help yourself . . . my pleasure . . . my privilege to let you drink it. (JIMMY *guzzles, growls, shakes his head.*)

JIMMY: Shit. Not much methylated spirit in that.

KING: The prices they charge at the restaurant –

JIMMY: This came from a restaurant –

KING: A French restaurant, in Dean Street –

JIMMY: Then it could be 60 per cent pure – (*He guzzles again.*) Maybe more . . . what is this . . .

KING: Cognac.

JIMMY: That's it then, what deceived me. I was expecting it to be a kinda brandy. Cognac you say, from Dean Street . . . well . . . now you alerted my expectations . . . let me *try* again. (*Guzzles more. A dog barks off.*)

KING: Did you hear that?

JIMMY: I heard something –

KING: Is that your whippet?

JIMMY: That's no whippet shit no. That's a Securicor dog . . . A guard dog, for the international container depot . . . they call them alsatians but I tell you something . . . the dogs those laddies use, they're not dogs . . . not when they're ferrying gold bullion for the Big Bangers to Japan, oh no. What you just heard then, my friend – that weren't an alsatian barking. That was a fucking wild wolf. From Alaska. They're not your run-of-the-mill Securicor alsatian, they are savage, untrained man eaters. From the wilds of Northern Antartica. (*The dog barks wildly in distance.*)

KING: You can tell?

JIMMY: Listen. That's one of them all right. They're killers, they're not proper dogs at all. The Brinks Matt robbers couldn't say 'Sit pal, here's a tin of Pedigree Chum Meat Chunks laced with arsenic gravy.' Oh no. Them animals wouldn't understand – they only speak Alaskan. (*KING starts to laugh.*)

KING: Who are you?

JIMMY: I used to work the Inter City from Glasgow to Euston . . . a steward.

KING: What you doing here in the middle of the night?

JIMMY: I live over there . . . Maryland Point . . . I come to look for dogs . . .

KING: If I may say so . . . it's a strange hobby . . . to come here in the middle of the night, looking for dead dogs . . .

JIMMY: Dead dogs! What do you think I am? Some kind of lunatic.

KING: You said –

JIMMY: I'm looking for live ones. To stop them getting killed. What do you take me for – some kind of dog undertaker.

KING: I meant no offence. (*Offers him bottle.*)

JIMMY (*drinking from it*): Christmas is the worst time . . . when they buy dogs for Christmas presents, little puppies for their kiddies then the novelty wears off . . . and they chuck them out of trains . . . to die on the train lines under the wheels . . . (KING *thinks about this, his own mood.*) I can't understand the mentality.

KING: It doesn't make sense.

JIMMY: I blame the booking office. I mean – wouldn't it strike you as unusual if some laddie came and said: 'Day return to Norwich, pal . . . and for me dog, make it just a one way ticket.'

KING: Cruel . . .

JIMMY: I blame the booking office clerks. Ever since they got kitted out with striped waistcoats they lost all sense of humanity, they think they're a fucking class apart . . . I thought you was a dog . . . I thought you was a dog that had been hit . . . I just saw the shadow crawling along the track . . . I thought you was an abandoned dog . . . (*Pause. KING is crying.*) What are you doing here, laddie?

KING: I'm a dog who got thrown out of a train . . .

JIMMY: Why you here, Mister?

KING: I came here tonight . . . because for every working day of my life for the last thirty five years . . . I came here . . . this was my depot . . . I was a driver, the Central Line.

JIMMY: The Central Line. I take my hat off to you my friend. That's not the fucking District Line, not the Upminister to Wimbledon run . . . the Central Line, I mean – I got respect for Central Line drivers . . . I don't know how you do it.

ING: Thirty five years.

MMY: I'm particularly referring to that bit east after Leytonstone when you go right for Hainault . . .

ING: Very easy to miss that turn. (*They're miming the LT map route, like slow motion dancers.*)

MMY: I bet there's been many a time a driver who's –

ING: The tricky bit is after South Woodford –

MMY: This is what I'm saying – if you get it wrong at the tricky bit after South Woodford . . .

ING: Instead of Roding Valley, Chigwell, Grange Hill, Hainault –

MMY: You could end up the other side of the world. (*They both roar with laughter, both drunken comrades.*)

ING: Or even worse . . . you could end up in Theydon Bois . . . (*Laughs.*) Or the real end of the world . . .

MMY: Where's that?

ING: Ongar! (*They both howl with laughter and shake hands warmly.* KING *changes mood, morose suddenly. Train goes past.*) All those passengers . . . on urgent missions . . . relatives dying . . . baby's being born . . .

MMY: Library books overdue –

ING: Who knows . . . What's your name?

MMY: Jimmy.

ING: Jimmy . . . tonight, it was a very special occasion . . . with my family . . .

MMY: I see you're dressed like a man with a very special occasion on his menu tonight . . .

ING: I retired. After thirty five years . . . hold my hands. (JIMMY *does so. They're sitting facing each other.*) In these hands . . . in thirty five years . . . how many lives did I hold in these hands . . . in thirty five years . . . (KING *moves* JIMMY's *hands like 'steering wheel.'*) No-one ever died

. . . when I was driving . . .

JIMMY: That's a honourable testament.

KING: Better than being punctual.

JIMMY: Best of both worlds I'd say.

KING: I'm being serious . . . winter Sunday afternoons . . . they were the time that I feared the most . . . all those empty platforms . . . just one figure at the far end of the tunnel as it gets dark. Brian Johnstone 'Down Your Way' on the radio, I was always scared that the wavering person on the platform . . . would . . . In front of my train. (*Pause.*) I wonder why none of them . . . ever did.

JIMMY: An eminent psychiatrist told me once, over a jug or two, on the midnight sleeper down from Aberdeen . . . he was a very eminent man indeed. He came from Finland, or Sweden or Islington. Some place like that. Anyway, what he told me was . . . suicides, they usually decide to kill themselves because someone shouted at them in the morning.

KING: She never raised her voice –

JIMMY: What I'm saying is –

KING: She didn't shout at me –

JIMMY: Who?

KING: My daughter, when she abused me tonight – she didn't even look at me. She just turned her head and walked away for ever.

STEVIE *is now there.*

STEVIE: That's not true, Mister King.

JIMMY: Who the hell are you – if you're a greyhound thiever for the Walthamstow syndicate, I tell you what I told Mister Raymond. A whippet is a whippet. And you don't need them in Walthamstow, especially when they come from Antartica. (*Pause.*)

STEVIE: What are you talking about?

JIMMY: Who the hell are you? Straight question, straight reply.

STEVIE: Mister King, I thought I might find you here . . . I've come to take you home . . . I got the car, I've come to take you home . . .

KING: Stevie, Stevie . . . thank you Stevie. This is (*To* JIMMY.) This young chap here, this is –

JIMMY: Stevie?

STEVIE: Right.

KING: Thank you Stevie . . . I appreciate your –

JIMMY: He your son?

STEVIE: Pardon?

JIMMY: You must be his son, I see a certain . . . family characteristic features and that.

KING: He's not my son. I have no son. I had two daughters.

JIMMY: Then you're a luckier man than me – I thought you was his son –

KING: My older daughter, he's her fiancé.

JIMMY: I should be so fortunate. I had a son . . . he was straight down the line, salt of the earth. Then he went to bleeding Reading University. Social Studies. Need I say more?

STEVIE: I want to take Mister King home.

JIMMY: All I'm saying is, how would you feel if your own flesh and blood, at the degree presentation ceremony at Reading University – your own son says: meet me room mate. And kisses it. Calls it Murray – I tell you, made bloody Boy George look like a twenty ton Japanese Sumi wrestler. The shame and the scandal –

STEVIE: I'm taking Mister King home, pal.

KING: I know what he's saying.

STEVIE: The car's just –

JIMMY: Yeah. He knows what I'm saying.

KING: Families. A man chooses his friends. His family is chosen for him. That's the shame of it all . . . that's the tragedy.

Dog barks off.

JIMMY: That sounds like my Jody. That's him. I gotta go . . . (*To* STEVIE.) Will he be all right?

KING: I'll be all right . . . Stevie, he's my daughter's fiancé . . .

JIMMY: Jody! Where are you, you little bugger!

JIMMY *exits.*

KING: You found me here . . .

STEVIE: The first place I come to look for you after I took Linda to the house.

KING: All my working life here . . .

STEVIE: I know. You're cold . . . better come home, I got the car – get warm . . .

KING: Wait . . . they gave me this when I retired . . . (*Shows watch.*) Six functions –

STEVIE: I know, you showed it to me . . .

KING: I took it off tonight . . . I shouldn't have put it on . . . because when I put it on this afternoon . . . I had to take off the watch my Malley gave me . . . my Malley . . .

STEVIE: I know who she is . . .

KING: I miss her so badly. (*He sobs.*) If she was here, tonight would have been so . . . so . . . so . . . different. (*Real heartbreaking sobs.* STEVIE *comforts him.*) Real things . . . real things . . .

STEVIE: Hey, Mister King . . . why don't we . . .

KING: Six functions . . . you'd never believe no-one could put so many things into something so small . . . I put it here . . . (*He places watch on line downstage.*) In 45 seconds comes the fish train to Liverpool street . . . in a millionth of a second, the watch – all those functions –

STEVIE: Nothing . . .

KING: A colleague of mine, he told me what it was like as he approached the man . . . at the end of the platform on the Sunday afternoon . . . and my colleague said he knew . . . before it happened . . . because the man looked up, and their eyes met, the second before he died under the wheels of my colleague's train . . . Susan never looked into my eyes . . . everything I believe in –

He tries to dart in front of thundering express train: devastating noise and flashing shadows and wind. KING *is swaying, held by his elbow by* STEVIE *as train goes.*

STEVIE: You can't give away your house, Mister King.

KING: You're holding my arm.

They look into each other's eyes. A long pause. Then STEVIE *bends to inspect pieces of shattered watch on the line.*

STEVIE: This ain't gonna play The Yellow Rose of Texas no more . . .

KING: I got nowhere to go.

STEVIE: You got your house.

KING: I gave it to my . . . other daughter.

STEVIE: Let's go to her. Tear up the contract. You don't really want to live in Trinidad the rest of your life, do you?

KING: I don't . . . don't want to be on my own.

STEVIE: You've been here for thirty five years, man. Too long to go back there. You don't know it – it's a different planet. You can't turn the clock back.

KING: My sister Rose and I . . . we have exchanged letters all those years . . .

STEVIE: Letters are a different world. Trinidad is – as different as England was when you first set foot here.

KING: You been there?

STEVIE: I was born there, Mister King. (*They eye each other again.* STEVIE *is leading* KING *away from train lines.*) I hope you're not offended that I talk to you like this but –

KING: What are you saying to me?

STEVIE: You can't give away your house, Mister King. And you can't sell it. If you went back to Trinidad with sixty five grand in your baggage . . . how could it be the same? You'd be a rich man . . .

KING: Where can I go?

STEVIE: I think you should stay here . . . with your daughters.

KING: I have only one daughter . . . Linda.

STEVIE: Let's go to the car . . . and talk to her when we get you home . . .

KING: Home!

KING *alone in spotlight. He removes overcoat he has been wearing this scene to reveal the London Transport Uniform underneath. Direct Address.*

It hasn't been a proper home . . . not since Malley died . . . I had no idea it was so near the end . . . if I had known it was nearly the end . . . so many things I would have said . . . Everyone in the hospital seemed to know . . . their eyes told me . . . they knew . . . I didn't see . . . I didn't see what they were saying even until the last time I went to see Malley in the hospital . . . Just before six o'clock in the evening, the 17th of September . . . I was early . . .

Scene Two

The Hospital.

KING *stands with newly washed and ironed nightdress. In his uniform, now with peaked cap.*

Enter Male DOCTOR.

DOCTOR: Mister King, isn't it?

KING: Yes. They told me to wait here . . . not just go straight into the ward, they said here. Malley, that's my wife . . .

DOCTOR: I'm sorry to have to tell you this, Mister King . . . but a little while ago, before you got here, your wife passed away. (*Pause.* KING *stunned, confused.*) She's at peace now. The suffering is over. (KING *bows head and starts to pray.* DOCTOR *wrings his hands.*) I know it's not easy . . . I mean . . . however much one tries to prepare oneself for it . . .

KING: Why didn't you tell me?

DOCTOR: Tell you?

KING: That she might die?

DOCTOR: I thought you had been told –

KING: No-one told me. No-one told me!

DOCTOR: But . . . couldn't you see she was dying?

KING: Why didn't you tell me?

DOCTOR: I thought you could see . . . (KING *sobs. Pause as he does so.*) I really don't know what to say, Mister King. It's always difficult.

KING: Our youngest daughter . . . she wants to be a nurse.

DOCTOR: Does she?

KING: My Susan.

DOCTOR: She's already here . . . she came after school . . .

KING: Susan?

DOCTOR: Yes.

KING: After school . . . was she here when . . .?

DOCTOR: I think . . . she was. Would you like a cup of tea . . .?

KING: I'd like to see Malley . . . I brought her clean nightdress . . .

KING *now sees* SUSAN, *in school uniform, standing by hospital bed.* KING *stands beside her. He has recovered his dignity and places parental arm on her shoulder.*

SUSAN: I don't know what to say, dad . . .

KING: You were here . . .

SUSAN: I just looked in after school . . . on the way home . . .

KING: I'm glad you were here. She wasn't alone.

SUSAN: She's at peace now.

KING: Susan . . . if you really want to be a nurse . . . you be a nurse.

SUSAN: Yes.

KING: Where's your sister, she should be here now.

SUSAN: I think she's going out tonight, dad. I left a note for her at home . . .

KING: She should be here now.

Fade to darkness.

Loud music before lights up on:

Scene Three

The living room of KING's *house in Stratford. Night. Music blaring from* LINDA's *ghetto blaster. She wears her fur and is furious. She opens the door to* STEVIE. *They bellow at each other – but we can't hear until* STEVIE *turns off the music.*

STEVIE: For God's sake, Linda.

LINDA: A little bit of music, to keep me company while I waited here –

STEVIE: You're waking half the damned street –

LINDA: Sod the street. Well, did you find him.

STEVIE: I found him. He's a bit confused. He's coming . . . he's in the car, he's er . . .

LINDA: Where did you find him?

STEVIE: He's very shocked, you know – when he heard that racket. After midnight.

LINDA: I said, where did you find him.

STEVIE: In the shunting yard at Stratford station.

LINDA: Where else! Of course . . . (*Tenderly.*) I'm glad you found him . . . is he all right?

STEVIE: He's cold . . . and he's very confused and . . . very humble, so go easy on the old man, Linda . . . please. (KING *shuffles in. Overcoat crumpled. Long pause. Then he goes to ghetto blaster and touches it.*)

KING: Linda, your behaviour tonight leaves a lot to be desired –

LINDA: What did he say?

KING: I said: Your behaviour and lack of consideration for my neighbours is intolerable. I could hear the music before we turned into the street. I forbid you to –

LINDA: Oi, oi. Wait a minute, daddy. If anyone should be offended –

STEVIE: Linda –

KING: Have you no consideration? What about Mrs Dwyer next door?

LINDA: What about the nosey old cow –

STEVIE: Linda!

KING: She probably had a seizure and fell out of bed, that noise. I will not permit it.

LINDA *goes to machine, looks at* KING, *turns up volume and switches on tape. Deafening music.* KING *holds hands over his ears and shudders.* STEVIE *turns it off.*

STEVIE: OK Linda, you made the point.

LINDA: Daddy, why don't you sit down. And what on earth have you been doing, staggering around in the middle of the night in a shunting yard? Look at the state of you. You stink like a distillery! How much have you drunk today?

KING: Linda, please. This is a most peculiar day. I'm so muddled . . . so muddled . . .

LINDA: I thought something terrible had happened to you. (*She helps him sit in armchair.*)

KING: Might have done, if Stevie hadn't so kindly –

LINDA: Oh very, very kind of Stevie. I'd been sitting here waiting to go home with Stevie when he set off to look for you. Do you know what the time is?

STEVIE: His watch got broken.

LINDA (*laughs, claps hands*): Mister hundred per cent punctuality! No watch –

KING: I got a watch . . . the one your mother gave me . . .

He settles in armchair. Finds the watch in his pocket. STEVIE *aside to* LINDA.

STEVIE: Take it easy, he's in a bad way.

LINDA: I can play music if I want to.

STEVIE: The old blind lady next door.

LINDA: What I do is up to me. Not Mrs Dwyer. Anyway, he exaggerates. She's not blind.

KING: She's not deaf . . .

LINDA: No, daddy. Do you want something . . . black coffee or something.

STEVIE: Linda, your father and me, we been talking –

KING: What Stevie said –

LINDA: Oh, Stevie now is it? A couple of hours ago it was Thingy-whatsisname.

STEVIE: That was before we got to know each other –

LINDA: And before you paid for the meal. Nice of you to walk out and let Stevie pay for it daddy. Not to mention taking away a fifty quid bottle of Remy Martin!

KING: The money, the money for the meal – I've got the money. I went to the Co-op bank before the –

He rummages in pocket. STEVIE *pats his shoulder.*

STEVIE: Forget it tonight Mr King. Linda, what me and your father were talking about was . . . whether it's such a good idea, him going back home to Trinidad.

LINDA: Pardon me?

STEVIE: You heard me sister. Whether he should return –

KING: What Stevie was saying to me was –

LINDA: What exactly *was* Stevie saying?

KING: He made it clear . . . that after all, after all these years . . . this is my home. Here. With you.

LINDA: With who?

STEVIE: You.

LINDA: Me?

KING: My daughter.

LINDA: You want to live here with me?

KING: I mean . . . I want to live in my own house. Here. This house.

LINDA: *This* house!?

STEVIE: Come on Linda . . . we've got the flat in Tooting.

LINDA: And now I've also got a house of my own. This house. I think dad'll love it going back on Wednesday – he's all packed. (*Indicates trunk.*) And Auntie Rose is so looking forward to him going there. You can't let him down, daddy. And all that sunshine, it'll be good for you. The winters here – old people die of the cold in England in the winter. I'm just thinking about your health, daddy.

KING: I much appreciate that, Linda –

STEVIE: Let's cut the crap. I think he'll be making a mistake. That's my opinion –

LINDA: And he's my father, so shut your mouth. My father is perfectly capable of making up his own mind.

STEVIE: Bullshit! Give him back the contract so he can think it over again in his own good time.

LINDA: Give him back what?

KING: Linda . . . what Stevie means is . . . I think I might perhaps have acted a little impetuously when I –

LINDA: You didn't, daddy. No way.

STEVIE: For God's sake, give him the deeds, Linda.

KING: I was angry and I –

LINDA: But daddy, darling. You'll be leaving the house to me when you die . . . so what difference does it make a bit earlier . . . letting me have it now.

STEVIE: The man's got to live somewhere for Christ's sake. He stays here, he's got to live –

LINDA: He could live with old Mrs Dwyer next door! She makes him lovely scarves . . . look (*Twirls it like a menacing whip.*) That'd be nice, wouldn't it daddy. You and old Mrs Dwyer next door keeping each other company –

KING: What I did tonight . . . it was in a moment of madness Linda and I now wish to withdraw the offer so –

LINDA: Offer, offer? This ain't no offer, father. This is a legal document signed sealed and delivered. The Woolwich Building Society solicitor in Ilford – you can't get much more legally binding than that. It's done. It's over.

STEVIE: Give me your handbag, woman.

LINDA: Get your hands off that, man. It is mine.

STEVIE: Linda, I swear to God I will hit you if you – (*They tug bag.*)

LINDA: Take your hands off me, you take your hands off me – (*She wins bag.*)

KING: Please, please, both of yous . . . don't fight. There's been enough misery tonight. Linda, please . . . for the love of your old dad . . .

LINDA (*laughs*): For what? Who? Who's he talking about . . . Love of . . . I could never love an Uncle Tom, dad. Not a fucking pathetic Uncle Tom.

STEVIE: Hold your tongue, woman.

KING: You owe me this much . . .

LINDA: The only thing I owe you, daddy . . . the only thing I'm grateful to you for is . . . that you taught me never to be humble like you. Humble humble, grateful, humble humble you.

KING: What's she saying? I don't understand what she's saying . . . what's she talking about?

LINDA: This house, daddy . . . this shit hole house . . . this big deal of yours . . . you know something? I can't wait to sell it, and buy somewhere decent. Because what this house reminds me of is all your years of grovelling and your gratefulness. You were the Uncle Tom to end all Uncle Toms . . . I was ashamed of you. Mum couldn't bear it neither. So bloody grateful always, you . . . you were the gift horse to every con-man who ever stepped in to this street. You gave a couple of bob to blind men who could see well enough to say: 'make it half a quid, guv. God bless you gov. What a gentleman!' You were the only stupid one who was still giving a Christmas tip to the milkman three years after he'd stopped his milk round. And when mum said anything, about still tipping the old milkie you said: What did you say? You said: 'Be grateful. This is the only country in the world that has such a reliable and punctual delivery service!'

In her fury, she hurls vase of SUSAN's *flowers to the floor. Vase smashes.*

KING (*holds hands over his ears*): Linda, Linda, I don't want to listen –

LINDA: And when at the school . . .

they called me nigger . . .

KING: Don't, Linda, don't. (*She kneels in front of him; face to face.*)

LINDA: *Please* don't. Where's your manners Mister King? You're a guest in my house now. When they called me nigger – nigger. Bath in black ink? Ha ha. What colour is it inside, ha ha. Is it black inside? Ha ha. Nigger girls are cock-suckers all right. They go like fucking rattle snakes, ha ha. When they chucked bricks at me in the park, when the white boys chucked bottles at me and Susan in the market coming back from bible class . . . I wanted you to react. Do something. When those white boys threw stones and kicked me and Susan and I told you, I wanted you to smash their yellow teeth down their skinny, smelly throats. Then I would . . . and Susan would and mum would have felt something for you instead . . . of contempt . . . But what was your attitude? 'They're ignorant,' you said. 'Turn the other cheek,' you said. You turned the other cheek all right, Mister. And you stuck a fluorescent sign on it. Kick my nigger arse. Well, I ain't turning the other cheek and I ain't giving you this back neither! (*Clutching handbag she runs out, into the street, banging front door closed behind her. Sound of her running high heels into distance. KING shakes and shudders and whimpers.*)

KING: Her anger . . . such anger. Have you ever known such rage? I have never been that full of hate . . .

STEVIE: Never?

KING: There were times, bad times . . . I'll not deny there were. But I always looked forward to . . . better things.

STEVIE: Then maybe, sometimes, you should have got angry . . .

He starts to clear up the debris. He holds the baby's breath flowers: KING takes them during the following: He and STEVIE are very close together.

There was a time when I behaved, oh sure. And I kept quiet and I kept my head down. But then one day come and I started to think: why am I doing this? To be accepted? Be grateful that they accept me, a black man? I'd have been assimilated. I was losing my self respect. So I looked at myself, and I saw the truth. (*Pause.*)

KING: You're young. I'm an old man. I'm an old age pensioner with a bus pass, and that's the truth.

STEVIE: I respect you, Mister King. When you start feeling sorry for yourself – Then I got no respect . . .

KING: Respect: I come from a line of people noted for respect, respect for authority, respect for our elders, and in those days, that was all part of respect for the Union Jack. When I first came here, to tell you the truth . . . there were hostilities . . . yes, which in those days . . . us men on the boat – with our black skin, we had no idea . . . the colour of our skin would matter. Because, it was after the war . . . and many of the men were expecting . . . almost a hero's welcome home, to England – the Mother Country. Ten thousand West Indians had fought the British War against Hitler. War heroes. They laid down their lives, spilled their blood. Died in burning planes over Germany. When I saw the film 'The Dambusters . . . there was not one black face. When we came home here to England . . . we hadn't been warned it wasn't really our home at all. The hatred here . . . it never said in the travel brochures that the colour of our skin was going to matter.

STEVIE: Look, I gotta go now, find Linda . . .

KING: Tell her, the things she said – I know.

STEVIE: You look after yourself, Mister King.

KING: Perhaps I have been a fool. I behaved when I could see it was all wrong . . . because to not behave meant that blood will flow. I had to protect my family. Linda, she has gone, where has she gone?

STEVIE: We got a flat, we share, in Tooting. We live together Mr King. Like a man and wife. I think she never got around to tell you.

KING: I thought it an astonishing

coincidence that you both lived in Tooting . . .

STEVIE: She didn't tell you because she thought . . .

KING: What?

STEVIE: She didn't want to upset you. She respects your values . . .

KING: Will you marry my daughter?

STEVIE: I got a lot of hard thinking to do. I didn't know her Mr King; I'm glad I got to know you. (STEVIE *goes to doorway to leave.*)

KING (*twirling ring on his finger*): In the wedding service, I recall . . . With this ring . . . Stevie you must repeat these words after the priest he says, so you say, With this ring I thee wed, With my body, I thee worship And with all my worldly goods I thee endow . . . (STEVIE *has now gone.* KING *looks at the room – all his wordly goods.*) All my wordly goods. (*He puts on coat.*) Linda will keep my wordly goods. Because she hates me. Because she always knew I loved Susan the most. Susan is so like Malley. I love Linda, and I love Susan. So I must make my peace with Susan.

Scene Four

The Hospital, as before.

DOCTOR *in white coat watches* SUSAN, *still in dinner party dress, plus raincoat, closes patient's eyes and firms jaw. She turns, leaving DOCTOR. He comfortingly pats SUSAN as she comes down stage.* KING *is waiting for her.*

KING: Susan . . . I came to find you . . .

SUSAN: Oh dad. She died. It reminded me of the night –

KING: Your mother –

SUSAN: I really loved that lady . . . And I'm supposed to be professional, you know . . . only another patient with terminal CA.

KING: All those things you said.

SUSAN: Please, dad . . . I really can't handle this tonight . . .

KING: They are true . . . what you said . . .

SUSAN: Dad, you're going to make me cry . . . and I don't want to.

KING: I treated you so bad, Suzie so very, very bad. I wish to God . . . Wish to God Almighty I . . . I . . .

Pause. He hugs himself, shuddering, breathing heavily. SUSAN *keeps trying not to meet his eyes.*

SUSAN: You're shivering dad. (*He clasps her hand.*)

KING: Oh, God Almighty, God Almighty . . . I've been such a damned fool, such a blind man . . .

He shudders and heaves and cries quietly. Determinedly, she doesn't comfort him.

SUSAN: Have you got a match?

KING: What?

SUSAN: I've got a cigarette – something to light it with?

KING: You don't smoke.

SUSAN: Only now and again . . . after something like tonight . . . the night porter gives us a cigarette in case we need a smoke.

He searches pockets for match and in doing so finds watch MALLEY gave him.

KING: Your mother's –

SUSAN: I recognise it. It's lovely. The match?

He lights her cigarette.

KING: The things Linda said to me tonight. So much hate, hate – so vicious, what she said.

SUSAN: Really.

KING: I all my life tried to protect you all from having those emotions.

SUSAN: You can't protect by ignoring them. Refusing to admit they exist –

KING: I said . . . what did I always say: Remember the Bible, turn the other cheek . . . They're ignorant, ignore them I said . . . I perhaps ignored too much. (*Pause.*) Did Malley hate me for it? Hate me?

SUSAN: Hate you?

KING: Did your mother hate me for it?

SUSAN: Mum told me what it was like when you were first here . . . at the beginning. Those days . . . and she told me how harsh it was. How cruel it was . . . and she said . . . Your father endured it with such great dignity.

KING: She said that?

SUSAN: That's what she said.

KING: Great dignity.

SUSAN: Her very words.

KING: She never said that to me . . .

SUSAN: Oh dad, she said it to me . . . Dad, please . . . look at me when I'm talking to you . . . look at me . . . look in my eyes. I don't know what you want me to say. Please, let me tell you not what Mum said . . . let me tell you why I am proud of you. I'll tell you one moment . . . one Sunday, my first communion at the church. I think you never spent any money on yourself, or on mum . . . I think it all went into the home, the family . . . but all four of us looked so well dressed. Little white gloves, your suit and . . . shiny shoes and . . . I remember when we stood on the church porch and the priest shook your hand . . . feeling so proud of my dad. Such pride in our family.

She kisses his cheek.

KING: Will we meet again before I go?

SUSAN: Still Wednesday?

KING: Yes. Susan, when I go, when I go back will you write to me at your Auntie Rose's.

SUSAN: Mmm. And will you write to me?

KING: Yes.

LINDA: It'll be nice, getting letters from you.

KING: It'll be nice, getting letters from you.

SUSAN: I'd better go now –

KING: Where are you going now?

SUSAN: To the nurses home.

KING: Linda, she has the house. She has it all. This watch Malley gave me . . . I would like you to have it. I've got a new one. (*Pause. She accepts it.*)

SUSAN: Perhaps next summer, I'll come and visit you. See you and Trinidad.

KING: And perhaps . . . perhaps decide to stay?

SUSAN: No, dad. This is my country. England.

KING *watches her exit as lights slowly fade. Fade in Marley's* 'Redemption Song.'

'Redemption Song' *continues as curtain music.*

BASTARD ANGEL

For Ray

'The time has come. There's a tremendous
thunderstorm advancing on us. A mighty
storm is coming to freshen us up. It's
going to blow away all this idleness and
indifference.'

Anton Chekhov, *Three Sisters*

'O, a storm is threatening
My very life today
If I don't get some shelter
I'm gonna fade away.'

Mick Jagger/Keith Richard, *Gimme Shelter*

'Let's all raise a glass
To the rock stars of the past
Those that made it
Those that faded
Those that never even made the grade
And those we thought would never last.'

Raymond Douglas Davies,
You Can't Stop the Music

Bastard Angel was first presented by the Royal Shakespeare Company at the Warehouse Theatre, London on 23 January 1980 with the following cast

SHELLY	Charlotte Cornwell
ALUN	Alun Armstrong
MIKE	Andrew Dickson
HOWARD	Hugh Fraser
STEVE	Darryl Read
TREV	Donald Sumpter
CARYL	Cheryl Hall
BILL	Roger Sloman
MAX	Fred Pearson
RICKY	Georgette Lindsay
VAL	Jill Baker
JOYCE	Matyelok Gibbs
BILLY	Robin Davies
STANMORE	Clive Merrison

Directed by Bill Alexander
Designed by Douglas Heap
Lighting by Brian Wigney
Sound by John A. Leonard
Stage Manager Titus Grant
Deputy Stage Manager Diana Durant
Assistant Stage Manager Simon Hooper

1. BERLIN GIG January 1980, the first quarter of show.
2. ACT ONE Brighton Hotel room. April 1979.
3. BERLIN GIG The second quarter of the January 1980 show.
4. ACT TWO The house. June 1979.
Interval
5. ACT THREE The garden. November 1979.
6. BERLIN GIG The third quarter of the January 1980 show.
7. ACT FOUR The house. December 1979.
8. BERLIN GIG Last quarter of the January 1980 show.

Berlin gig January 1980.
The first quarter
Empty stage set for rock band. Sound of the
crowd building to fever. Dim light – we see
musicians taking up their places,
instruments.
Crowd sounds grow as the musicians tune
briefly.

VOICE on P.A.: THE ANGELS.
Sudden brilliant orange/red light. Explosion
of crowd noise.
The band run through a medley of the rock
numbers they may play.
A spotlight suddenly picks out stage left for
SHELLY's entrance.
Instead she bounds on stage right. She goes
to stage left talking to the musicians, half
dancing; she jumps about on the way to the
microphone centre stage.
She wears stage clothes. The band's tempo
mounts and leads into the first number intro.
Lights go to red.
The first number:

SHELLY: Well I pulled into Pittsburgh
rollin' down the Eastern seaboard
I got my diesel wound up and she's
running like never before
There's a speed zone ahead on the right
But I don't see a cop in sight
Six days on the road, and I'm gonna make
it home tonight.

The I.C.C. is checking in down the line,
I'm a little overweight and my log book's
way behind.
But nothing bothers me tonight, I'm
gonna dodge all the scales all right
Six days on the road, and I'm gonna make
it home tonight.

Well my rig's a little old but that don't
mean she's sold
There's a good thing blowin' from my
smokestack, black as coal,
My home town's coming in sight, and if
you think I'm happy, you're right,
Six days on the road, and I'm gonna make
it home tonight.

I've got ten forward gears and a George
overdrive,
I'm taking little white pills, and my eyes
are open wide,
I just passed Jimmy in white, you know
I'm passing everything tonight,
Six days on the road, and I'm gonna make
it home tonight.

Well it's been six days since I kissed my

baby goodbye,
I coulda had a lotta fun with a lotta other
guys,
Could have found one to hold me tight,
But I could never make believe it's all
right,
Six days on the road, and I'm gonna make
it home tonight.

Well I pulled into Pittsburg rollin' down
the Eastern seaboard
I got my diesel wound up and she's
running' like never before,
There's a speed zone ahead on the right
But I don't see a cop in sight,
Six days on the road, and I'm gonna make
it home tonight.

Danke, danke, sprechen sie Englische?
(*'Ja's' from the audience.*) Ich kann nicht
Deutsch sprechen, es tu mir sehr leid.
(*Laughter.*) Das ist sehr gut? Ja?
(*Laughter. She checks the band is ready.*)
I'd like to say how great it is to be here in
Berlin again. I'd like to say it – but I can't.
(*She laughs.*) After such a long, long
time. This gonna be good night tonight
then? We gonna have a good time. When
the revolution comes, you lot'll be the
first to go. But in the meantime let's have
a good time. Right? I can't hear you.
(*Audience cheer.*) Come on then – here
we go . . .

Intro of 'Here Comes the Night'. It stops
abruptly.

You don't want to hear that *now*, do you?
Not already. I mean, we've got all night
you know.

Fast aggressive intro of 'Rock 'n' Roll
Night'. She claps her hands above her
head to get the audience to join in. She
stomps around the stage during the intro.

We've played the sawdust pubs
And the late-night drinking clubs
A million bucks in L.A.
Played ghost town gigs with no P.A.
So why are we here still playing it?
Put it all down to rock 'n' roll – rock 'n'
roll, rock 'n' roll.

Must've played ten thousand places
Seen the world in staring faces
Slept in every gas station
Fifty states across the nation
Doesn't matter I survive
I get along on a song
If it's rock 'n' roll.

'Cos when the band is tight – when the
   band is tight
And the sound is right – and the sound is
   right
Then we're all gonna wanna rock and roll
tonight.
It's a rock 'n' roll night tonight
It's a rock 'n' roll night yeah
It's a rock 'n' roll night tonight
It's a rock 'n' roll night yeah
It's a rock 'n' roll night tonight.
It's a rockin'an'a rollin'
It's a night to lose your soul in
It's a rock 'n' roll night tonight.

I'm outa my head, way outa sight
'Cos it's a rock 'n' rollin night
Our brain cells dyin on the floor
And still they shout and scream for more
That's why we're still here doin it
Put it all down to rock 'n' roll – rock 'n'
   roll rock 'n' roll
We bin ripped off cheated undersold
Played out our lifetimes on the road
People laugh and they abuse
But you pay the bread so you can choose
Doesn't matter I survive
I get along on a song if it's rock 'n' roll.
Cos when the band is tight . . . etc

Immediate: 'Here Comes The Night' intro.

Well, here it comes,
Da da da da da

ALL: Da da da da da

SHELLY: Here comes the night, oh yeah
   Here comes the night
   I can see right outa my window
   Walking down the street
   My guy with some other girl
   His arms around her
   Like it used to be with me
   Oh, it makes me want to die
   Yeah, here it comes,
   Here comes the night.
   There they go
   Funny how they look so good together
   Wonder what is wrong with me?
   Why can't I accept the fact
   He's chosen her instead of me.
   Here comes the night
   Here it comes, oh yeah.
   He's with her; she's turning down the
   light
   Now she's holding him like I used to do.
   I can see her closing his eyes
   And telling him lies
   Like he told me, too

Here it comes
Oh yeah
Here comes the night,
Oh yeah
Here it comes again
Here comes the night.

*Instrumental. Repeat last verse and last
chorus fastest. Lights/sound
blackout*

Act One

April 1979.
Crowd sounds fade as lights go up on: a
hotel room in Brighton. Night. TREV *is*
urinating in a vase on the coffee table, room
centre. He is talking to someone in the
lavatory – the door is ajar, but TREV *shouts.*

TREV: Havoc, I tell you, it was havoc.
They're all fucking mad. She followed me
into the lavatory. She locks the door
behind her. This was at the Embassy,
remember.

VOICE: There isn't an Embassy in San
Francisco.

TREV: Nar, not the embassy – what do you
call them fucking places?

VOICE: Consulate.

TREV: It was the place you went, when
they busted you.

VOICE: The Consulate!

TREV: Yeah, this was at the consulate.
And they was all there in their fucking
dinner jackets and medals and
emulsioned false teeth, you know.
Passing round the fucking sherry, do you
mind, and these 'Britishers' – 'Britishers',
remember? (*Laughs.*) And she follows
me, don't she, upstairs into the fucking
lavatory. I thought she was just another
groupie. When I had her, how was I to
know she was the fucking ambassador's
daughter? How was I to know she was
fifteen, for Christ's sake? So I'd given her
the big E and at this do, she followed me
up into the lavatory, like, and she locks
the door and she says, 'Last time, before
you leave California.' I says, 'Fuck off –
you're under age. Anyway I come up here
for a shit and I can't shit in front of fifteen-
year-old ambassador's daughters. I'm
funny that way.'

VOICE: It was only a consulate.

TREV: She lifts up her skirt, no knickers. I
thought this is a bit fucking naff, know
what I mean. In a consulate like. At a
sherry party. So I climbs out of the
window. Forgot we'd gone upstairs.
That's how the ankle went. When I
landed.

He is about to zip up his flies. The sound of
the lavatory cistern and SHELLY *comes*
in from the lavatory, in a dressing-gown.

SHELLY: You'll kill the flowers.

TREV: I was bursting – the dubes, keep
pissing.

SHELLY (*lifts the vase*): Taking all this new
wave a bit far, aren't you? (*Pause.*) I
mean, these are daffodils.

SHELLY *takes the vase to the lavatory*
and returns with it empty. In the other
hand she has the flowers which she forgets
to return to the vase. She switches on the
T.V. A whine. No picture.

Midnight! Nowhere to go and nothing on
TV. This must be England. (*Goes to*
video cassettes.) Casablanca or The
Muppets?

TREV: And I lands in this fucking stable, or
something. In the yard. Pitch black.
Where I landed. Ankle on fire and I was
throwing up all the tortillas –

SHELLY: The Taqueria la Cumbre on
Valencia?

TREV: Where we'd been!

SHELLY: Where else! I got The French
Connection, but after an hour there's ten
minutes of you on Top of the Pops –

TREV: Ten minutes?

SHELLY: I was laughing so much, I forgot
to switch it off when Blondie come on.

TREV: Her head's so big . . . I mean,
literally, like she should be six feet six for
a head that size.

SHELLY: The Maltese Falcon – let's have
The Maltese Falcon, yeah?

TREV (*prevents her putting on the cassette*):
The ambassador comes out, I mean, it
musta looked a bit peculiar, me going in
the Kharzie and her coming out. He's got
this fucking gun, shotgun, and he's in this
white dinner jacket and medals and . . .
I'm all over the place, last night of the
tour, like, and bit of dust and smack and
. . . he sticks this gun up me hooter and
stares, real hate, you know, real fucking
hate you could put in a salami slicer and I
says: 'Come off it, Sir Roger'. His name,
see. I says, 'you can't shoot me, you
cannot. I'm in the band. I'm a celebrity.
I'm a Britisher. That's why you're having
this sherry party like. For us, for me.' He
looks so snotty, you know. Right snotty
posh voice, he says: 'Inside the consulate

I am obliged to treat you as a distinguished visitor in California enhancing the dignity of Her Majesty's Government and aiding its coffers. But we are in a backyard and outside the realm and I am justified in treating you like the little asshole mother fucking shit you are.' Yeah . . . nice, isn't it? Nice way for an ambassador to treat his fucking distinguished guest.

SHELLY: What are you doing in Brighton on a wet Wednesday night in April?

TREV: I came to see the show.

SHELLY: What did you think?

TREV: Great. Great, I mean ace. Really great show.

Pause.

You don't do the full medley now.

SHELLY: We only do all the oldies abroad now.

TREV: Europe in a fortnight –

SHELLY (*self-mocking*): We're on juke boxes in every freeway service station in Belgium, I believe.

They laugh.

Lot going in Germany. Very big in the small towns.

They laugh again.

TREV: We haven't done a thing in Germany – well, maybe that figures. Kraut rock.

SHELLY: Maybe –

TREV: What?

SHELLY: There's some talk of us doing Berlin again.

TREV: Berlin, great. What . . . seven, eight years?

SHELLY: That was the last time. 72ish.

TREV: I sorta thought –

SHELLY: Not for eight years. They say they're keen to have us – to wind up the European tour in Berlin.

TREV: Bowie's left there now, ain't he? Or was that Munich?

SHELLY: Vienna. Nice to see you, Trev.

TREV: You didn't stay for the –

SHELLY: No.

TREV: When they said you'd be back at the hotel – not gone home. The guys –

SHELLY: They'll be over after the raffle. Lot of chicks. Tonight. Fucking boring students from the university. I hate students.

TREV: I wondered, you know, if you –

SHELLY: Headache.

TREV: Still get them?

SHELLY *smiles. She drinks a fast cognac. She rolls a joint.*

SHELLY: They're psychosomatic. These migraines. It's all in my head. Did you take her out first. The California chick?

TREV: How do you mean?

SHELLY: You always said; 'Not straight to bed, let's go out first, have a dance'. I liked that.

TREV: Bit too old for all that. I need me five hours now.

SHELLY: Now!

TREV: I never treated anyone else like I treated you. You were special. You paid me wages! (*Pause.*) I was telling them, where was that place you chucked that what's name out – thought he was a fucking groupie?

SHELLY: Sheffield. What was Terence Stamp doing in Sheffield?

TREV: I wonder what he's doing now?

SHELLY: Last week, in . . . Ipswich, I saw someone who looked . . . looked incredibly like him. Not whatever he looked like then, but what, how he must look now . . . now. And his mate looked a bit like David . . . actually.

TREV: Hear from David?

SHELLY: Me accountants do. (*Laughs.*)

SHELLY *passes the joint to* TREV. *He inhales deeply.*

TREV: Our accountant said: Shit, you guys must be hard up. Band here needs some bread – four boys sharing the same fag. (*Laughs.*) Nar, seriously it was a really good show. Wound 'em up at the start. Over an hour late going on – they were screaming for your blood.

SHELLY: New roadies. Lost the way.

TREV: You kidding – to Brighton? That's Monty Python.

SHELLY: I dunno where Pete gets them – kids. We were all a bit pissed by the time –

TREV: You should have explained the hold-up.

SHELLY: I wanted to see if I could . . . get them back.

TREV: You fucking did.

SHELLY: I didn't think I was going to. The others were getting wound up – Alun was out of his head.

TREV: I noticed. Made a change. Still, he never fell off the stage tonight.

SHELLY: All kids . . . what about at the back?

TREV: Lots of kids. Students, mainly.

SHELLY: I wonder how they've even heard of half the stuff they was asking for.

TREV: At the front –

SHELLY: There was a boy, couldn't have been born when it came out. He kept asking for an oldie. So I never did it.

TREV: Why didn't you do it?

SHELLY: I made out I never heard him. (*Laughs.*) Ignorant fuckers! I saw John Lennon –

TREV: Here?

SHELLY: Nar in New York. I wanted to touch him.

Pause.

TREV: He's really retired.

SHELLY: I really . . . love . . . that last album. I love it so much I can't even play it now.

She snatches back the dope.

Melody Maker still love *you*.

TREV: Only us and The Police – they *all* like us.

SHELLY: How does he keep vomiting over the microphone?

TREV: Drinks salt water. In the lager cans, ain't lager – it's salt water, see.

SHELLY: I wondered. Ah . . . (*Smokes.*)

TREV: But he really has got some bottle, you know. At Madison Square Garden, he did . . . you'll never believe this – he did twenty-five minutes. Yeah! Twenty-five minutes – Bob Seeger did two and a half fucking hours. Van Morrison night before did Madame George four times, cause he reckoned he couldn't get it right. Him, he does twenty-five minutes and pulled the plugs. Going off, havoc, honest to God, I thought there was going to be murder, he turns round and he says: 'Ever feel you've been cheated?' The cunts loved it, they fucking loved it.

SHELLY: Ed's tactics?

TREV: He should have told *us*. Patti Smith did three and a half hours and when they pulled her plugs she kept playing with bleeding fingers until the last string broke. He did twenty-five minutes. Shot to number four over night.

SHELLY (*sorting through video cassettes*): Shall we have The Maltese Falcon?

TREV: The News of the World.

Pause.

Have you heard –

SHELLY: It's a Sunday newspaper.

TREV: Heard about them and me?

SHELLY: Thought there must be a reason you showed up.

TREV: Look, I don't wanna blow it for everyone.

SHELLY: How's that?

TREV: See Shelly, they know how old I am.

SHELLY: Eh?

TREV: They're going to expose me. In the News of the World.

SHELLY: Centre page spread?

TREV: I'll have had it. On Sunday, this Sunday I think, the News of the World are going to reveal it – that I'm forty. In October. (*Pause.*) I'm supposed to be twenty-two. (*Pause.*) They don't know about me houses yet. (*Pause.*) I dunno. They don't believe I've been on the dole all me life and live in a seventeen storey council flat in Kennington. With me mum and dad.

SHELLY: Do they know he's dead?

TREV: I think she may have given them a photo of me with me kids. Illona might've. I dunno if it's her who's busted me.

SHELLY: She wouldn't grass on you – she needs the alimony.

TREV: She reckons she can fuck me up and still have it. She's incredibly mad about that Swede.

SHELLY: Still?

TREV: Yeah. And you. Smashed the TV when you were on.

SHELLY: What's Ed make of it?

TREV: Christ, I ain't told Ed. Leave it out.

SHELLY: He knows you were with me right . . . way back, mid-sixties even – you weren't twelve then, for fuck's sake.

TREV: 'Course he knows it, but he'll deny it. Stands to reason.

SHELLY: It needed you to hold them together; he *needs* you.

TREV: Yeah . . . but thirty-nine, you know.

SHELLY: Ditch you? They couldn't handle it without you!

TREV: Always get another drummer.

SHELLY: Set them off and –

TREV: Like a rocket when it's run out of gunpowder?

SHELLY: You can't like playing their shit.

TREV: We are the only British punk band to make it in America! The only one – who's heard of The Boomtown Rats in Santa Fe?

She lights the joint again.

SHELLY: Everyone knew you lot were fucking . . . phoney. I dunno how no-one blew it sooner.

TREV: No-one wants the illusion smashed. The dream spiked. The kids, they *liked* me, you know. I . . . err . . . what am I gonna do?

SHELLY: I wish there was something on TV . . . something . . . not a cassette but something . . . unexpected.

TREV: They had this Noel Coward movie on every night in California. The same movie. City by city, the same late night movie. First three nights, I thought – what a fucking coincidence. Same movie every time I turn it on. All these different stations showing it, each time I drop off – next night I pick it up in a different city four hundred miles away. The one with the ghost –

SHELLY: I saw it on T.V.

TREV: It was like going backwards. On the plane, over the pole, when one minute it's pitch dark and the next dazzling sunshine on the snow. I never kip that bit – I ask them to wake me up.

SHELLY: You could still be thirty-eight if you flew to L.A. four times a week.

Pause.

TREV: Nothing I can do, is there?

Pause.

SHELLY: I wished you'd stayed with us. I really do. Miss you, still.

TREV: Steve's great – he's very good, you know. I didn't realise when he was with them that he was that good.

SHELLY: You were better – you were in from the start. Drums and vocals – that's what it's about. You and me –

TREV: I got fed up – if I hadn't been screwed on the divorce with the houses, I'd have stayed. I wanted to be so broke she wouldn't get a fucking penny.

SHELLY: That's why you joined them?

TREV: How was I to know they'd make it? I thought they were so fucking diabolical she'd starve for years.

Pause.

SHELLY: What did you think of our last album?

TREV: Good – too varied; but I liked it. A lot.

SHELLY: No promotion.

TREV: They're stupid cunts.

SHELLY: We didn't make the Beeb play list. They never banned your new single! Played it!

TREV: That's why we never went above seven. If the News of the World blows it . . . we'll find we're being played by Diddy Fucking David Hamilton.

SHELLY: You don't look forty – bluff it!

TREV: I'd like to say how nice it is to be forty. I'd like to be able to say it, but I can't.

Pause. They laugh. Another joint is lit. SHELLY *swallows some pills and sips Cognac.*

Ed'll sue me or something – more lawyers than Goldenballs.

SHELLY: He couldn't –

TREV: They're all so . . . moral. Pure, that's the word, like the best Bolivian snow. Fanatical about . . . being real. That's why it ain't rock'n'roll. That Sham 69 bloke – he's a cross between Bruce Forsyth and Billy Fucking Graham.

CARYL comes in. She is younger than SHELLY.

CARYL: They want . . . two nights next time.

SHELLY: Good.

CARYL: Trev – hey, you get it?

TREV: Caryl, how are you? Long time no see!

CARYL: Come on, you got it?

TREV: Caryl, I have bad news.

CARYL: O, Shelly – he's here.

SHELLY: Bill? Here now?

CARYL: In the foyer.

SHELLY: When did he get here?

CARYL: Only just.

SHELLY: Did he see the show?

CARYL: I don't think so – he didn't say. Come on Trev, don't keep me hanging on: well?

TREV: You'd better sit down, Caryl. I got some bad news for you.

CARYL: Don't piss me about.

TREV: Caryl, honest – my mother's life, I tried so hard to bring you a few lines.

CARYL: Busted at customs?

TREV: No. I never had none. Caryl, I tell you I tried everywhere and I couldn't get it.

CARYL: You was in L.A. for three fucking days –

TREV: That's true.

CARYL: End of tour. The last three nights.

TREV: Caryl, it's different since you were there – it's all changed. In L.A. you cannot get cocaine for life or money. You just can't get the stuff. There's a shortage of it in L.A. There's nowt.

Pause.

Honest. Ain't that right Shelly?

SHELLY *doesn't hear; she's poking an ear, wriggling it, inspecting wax. Puts on make-up.*

CARYL: You lying cunt. You liar. Mother fucking liar – L.A.'s like a sherbet dip, it's like dandruff – instead of shaking hands they have to rub noses to get the feeling back. I only need just a few toots.

She lunges at him.

TREV: Leave it out, leave it out. I'm an old man. 'Course I got it – here.

CARYL (*grabs it frantically*): You cunt. (*She opens the foil.*) Hey – you cunt. (*Laughs.*) Is this good? It's no fucking mixture?

TREV: Want a written guarantee?

CARYL: Is it good? It better be good.

TREV: I bought it off the pilot who flew it in up through Mexico. Hey, you know on the Mexican border the Yanks only got one plane? So the dealers fly in the dope in twelve planes at the same time. Always eleven get through. And the eleven pilots buy out the one who's caught. No wonder they lost Vietnam.

CARYL sits and prepares lines on a mirror during this.

Half the embassy are on it, you know. At some do in L.A. I met the President – *Life* President of some bank there; all he talked about was whether Linda Rondstat was gonna marry Brown. Sniffing as he spoke. Rondstat did a really good version of that whatsit – ooo, bint's name, Elvis Costello song.

CARYL: Allison.

TREV: Heard it?

SHELLY: No.

CARYL: Brahms and Gregorian chants. Shelly's favourites.

TREV: This geezer, *Life* president – dropped dead. Jogging in his lunch hour. Wild, eh, withdrawal symptoms on missing his macrobiotic. In San Francisco –

CARYL: You go to the Cafe Florré – that still good?

TREV: Where you think I got this?

CARYL: I liked watching the fags on a Friday night, changing out their labourers' . . . cowboy clothes . . . sitting on the sidewalk tables putting on their make up, and wigs and dresses.

TREV: It's total S and M now. A bar in Castro Street I had this thing who –

SHELLY (*suddenly*): It was . . . fantastic. (*Pause.*) Tonight it *was* really good. They were all bored and image and 'Where's the fucking Police' and . . . they begged me for more.

CARYL: Your car's ready.

SHELLY: I don't want to go back to London tonight. Can't we have a party?

CARYL: We could book the recreation room –

TREV: Well –

SHELLY: Is anyone here? Are the boys back?

CARYL: In the bar downstairs – a lot of spare.

SHELLY: Let's have a party. I mean, shall we?

CARYL: Bill wants to talk to you.

SHELLY: Now? O, well. (*Holds* CARYL's *arm.*) Don't toot no more – when I talk to him I want you to take notes. Shorthand.

CARYL: I'll get you the cassette.

SHELLY: No. He'll be more careful what he says if he sees you taking notes.

CARYL: Do you know what the fucking time is?

SHELLY: Caryl, you nicked a hundred quid outa the petty cash to score some smack, so I think you could –

CARYL: I'll pay it back. An advance, that's all.

SHELLY: Please. Since he's come here tonight . . .

CARYL *shrugs. She sighs loudly.*

CARYL: You want me to book the reception room *as well*?

SHELLY: Please.

CARYL: *And* send Bill up?

SHELLY: If you can handle both ordeals without any heavy psychiatric fees. You know.

CARYL: All right. (*She begins to go.*)

SHELLY: Caryl. Did you think we were good?

Pause.

CARYL: Yeah.

Pause.

SHELLY: Only, you never said.

CARYL: They enjoyed it. They told you. We sold a few T-shirts.

SHELLY: Did we?

CARYL: Just a few. And the boys are up. Buzzing.

SHELLY: They didn't say –

CARYL: They only tell you the truth when they think you're pissed.

SHELLY: When I go outa the dressing-room.

CARYL *goes.*

The house, see.

TREV: Getting it? I mean – is this it then?

SHELLY: If I can afford it.

TREV: If Bill can.

Pause. She laughs. She plays three chords on a guitar. Shouting and laughter off. She puts on sunglasses.

SHELLY: Listen to them. (*Laughs. Pause.*) I'm getting a lot of wax in my ears. (*Wiggles her finger.*) Look, I am sorry you know . . .

TREV: Me moaning, and you really up. Tonight.

SHELLY: Have another brandy – go on, have another brandy.

TREV: I gotta drive back.

SHELLY: One of the drivers'll take you back –

TREV: Angie'll get a bit, you know. First week off the road for –

SHELLY: I'll phone her.

TREV: *You* phone her? That'll really fuck her up. She is so jealous of you! (*Laughs.*) All right, I'll stay. But you gotta get me a driver.

SHELLY: I'll get Caryl to do it. No, I'll ask the desk downstairs meself.

HOWARD *enters. He has a champagne bottle.*

HOWARD: She's here again, Shelly.

SHELLY: Who – my double?

HOWARD: She'd done her hair like you. She's got identical clothes.

SHELLY (*laughs*): What's she trying to do? If it was to pull 'my admirers . . .' that'd make sense. But trying to screw me?

TREV: It'd be stereo masturbation. Hi ya then, sunshine.

HOWARD: Trev, I tell you – you're full of shit.

TREV: Listen, I got letters from some guy in Pentonville asking if I'm gonna get back to you 'cause if I don't he'll take me place. He's practising the old records and'll be out on parole in 1997.

SHELLY (*laughing, stoned*): I can't take it. What do I want all these dykey doubles for? (*Laughs.*) It's too much.

Enter ALUN. Greetings. He's dressed always in black. He takes brandy SHELLY is just pouring herself.

TREV: Old Black Magic himself.

ALUN: I am in mourning for my wife. Is she dead? No, that's why I am in mourning. The copper's here again.

SHELLY: I'm not letting him near me unless I have a metal detector. In Plymouth he locked me up with handcuffs and abused my body.

ALUN: They have to practise flagellation on someone before they go on duty.

TREV: I thought it was only schoolboys who abused your body now you're so old.

SHELLY: I've been told when I leap around on stage and the lights are red, I still look seventeen.

TREV: All those fucking schoolboys. What are they like now?

ALUN: They don't get their rocks off slicing up rabbits, that's for fucking sure.

SHELLY: They all wanna be sucked off. They want to cum in my mouth. I blame it on comprehensive education.

ALUN: I got a great B side for the election: When I fell in love with Margaret Thatcher
It wasn't a political choice.
It was lust I confess.
I got a hard on at the sound of her voice. Olé.

Silence.

Fuck you. I'll go down the pier and have a rub against the Laughing Policeman.

He exits.

TREV: He was off.

SHELLY: He's got problems.

TREV: Haven't we all.

SHELLY: Alun has a bad problem. Alun has the problem of being Alun. If he could be someone else he'd be OK.

Pause. Enter BILL, a middle-aged man, in immaculate clothes. Pause.

BILL: I thought you were wonderful Shelly. It was quite something out there.

SHELLY: We changed the opening.

BILL: I thought it was . . . just great.

SHELLY: The new stuff – what did you think worked best?

BILL: That's a difficult question. (*Clasps SHELLY.*) They're all great in different ways. You can't explain it.

SHELLY: A single – you hear one?

BILL: I heard four or five singles.

SHELLY: Did you see the show, Bill?

BILL: It was great. All of you were . . . really terrific. Hello . . .

SHELLY: You know Trev. He hasn't played with us for three years.

BILL: I'd never have believed it. You fitted back into it beautifully.

TREV: I wasn't playing.

Pause.

BILL: It sure was a great show.

Pause.

Shelly, if you can spare me a minute. Confidentially. I won't keep you from the festivities downstairs for too long.

TREV *looks at* SHELLY.

TREV: I'll see you in the recreation room then.

HOWARD: What'll I tell the bulging Y-fronts?

SHELLY: Ask one up for a drink. The kid who kept asking for – (*Slight hesitation.*) And Caryl – tell Caryl I'm talking to Bill.

TREV *and* HOWARD *go.* SHELLY *pours herself a drink.* BILL *declines.*

SHELLY (*slow talk now: she's stoned*): You should have seen the show Bill. The boys were . . . tight. The sound was good. It . . . came together.

BILL: I caught the last quarter. You gave them their money's worth.

SHELLY: We started late. Well . . . the house?

Pause. SHELLY *wiggles her finger in her ear.*

BILL: They accepted our offer.

SHELLY: How much did you go to?

BILL: Let me worry about the financial details. They were hoping for an Arab, so you can appreciate . . . the difficulties. It's been on the market for . . . well, let me just say it was an extremely complicated deal – it's always worse when you have to deal with the Official Receiver's Office. But they accepted, subject to the usual formalities. You can let me worry about all that. A month – two months . . . three months at the outside, certainly by the time you get back from the tour . . .

SHELLY: Yes?

BILL: Yes, you'll be the new owner.

Pause.

You don't look especially pleased.

SHELLY: Will *I* be the owner. Me?

BILL: The taxation situation, Shelly, is highly complex. But you *will* be the owner. Make no mistake, it'll be your house, although there might be some

readjustment to the publishing company – the house becoming the head office in the books, that sort of thing but . . . I'm working through the details with Hungerford. He's good.

SHELLY: Is he the one who did me personal . . . err – I mean the maintenance deal with David for the kids and . . . (*Pause.*)

BILL: I believe it was his partner. Property, that's Hungerford's thing –

SHELLY: So was the maintenance deal.

BILL: With the right contract, everyone can be satisfied. A good price before the market surges forward after the election.

Pause.

SHELLY (*earnest*): I really do want that house.

BILL: And all that land? There was a plan for an extension to the M11 which might have affected the orchards –

SHELLY: You'd better check that.

BILL: Morrison'll be going down to deal with it at first hand. At most it'll only impinge on a hundred yards or –

SHELLY: I don't want faces at my window. Peering in.

BILL: There's an acre of landscaped gardens in between the house and the orchards. You'll be secluded.

Pause.

So, if you'll agree to what I'm arranging in principle.

SHELLY: I'll get my accountant to check it.

BILL *smiles.*

BILL: I thought you'd be pleased. As your accountant, I am.

SHELLY: I know the garden. The layout. There's a pond.

BILL: Yes. And a stream.

SHELLY: In summer there's a lot of gnats.

BILL: It'll be nice, living in a house again. And in the country –

SHELLY: I'll be on my own.

BILL: There's a housekeeper and his wife in the house.

SHELLY: I saw them . . . when I had a look at it. They're staying?

BILL: They've got some rights, but if we offer the right price –

SHELLY: I want them to stay. (*Pause.*)

BILL: I know they've been there a long time, but –

SHELLY: I want them there!

BILL: . . . Well . . . of course.

SHELLY: I'll go and have another look when –

BILL: Wait until the contracts have gone through. I don't want you to get depressed if . . . if there's some hitch.

SHELLY: No hitches, Bill.

BILL: You worry about the music, I'll worry about the contract. Oh . . . you'll be in Europe. I could sign?

Pause.

SHELLY: I wish you'd seen us tonight. We were . . . really . . . good. A rock'n'roll show. You haven't got no rock'n'roll in you, Bill.

BILL: Nor's the Official Receiver.

SHELLY: It worked tonight. We were very together.

Pause.

BILL: I'm glad you're on form. Oslo and Stockholm – they were disappointed. But, welcome back. The European itinerary looks tough. Caryl should have the dates and travel arrangements before the end of the week. Oh, and the German promoter thinks Berlin are almost definitely in. Maybe even two nights.

SHELLY: Berlin?

BILL: After Amsterdam. To wrap it up.

SHELLY: I'll be very pleased if –

BILL: The house as well? To come back to, in June.

BILLY, *about sixteen, comes in.* BILL *looks at* BILLY *and then he looks at* SHELLY. BILLY *looks around as though bored.* BILL *goes out.* BILLY *goes to* SHELLY: *she strokes his hair. She is quite drunk and stoned. She sways and slumps in the chair.*

SHELLY: How do you know . . . All the old old old old ones? Hey, mind. I'm going to drop this bottle.

She drops the bottle. He kneels beside her. Shouting and laughter off.

GIRL VOICE OVER: If you think I'm going to have that bloody great thing –

SHELLY *begins to laugh. She moves her hand up and down the neck of the bottle as though masturbating it. She looks directly at* BILLY. *Silence.* BILLY *opens* SHELLY's *dressing-gown and kisses a breast.* CARYL *comes in. Pause.*

CARYL: Oh . . .

SHELLY: Perks of the job, Caryl. I'm a rock'n'roll star.

CARYL *goes. Pause.*

Haven't you got a tongue in your head? I'm a rock'n' roll star.

As lights fade: fade in long guitar intro of 'So You Wanna be a Rock'n'Roll Star'.

Berlin gig January 1980
The second quarter
The band in bright light play long spectacular intro of 'Rock'n'Roll Star' waiting for SHELLY.
She enters in stage clothes, drinking from a bottle which she puts down upstage before getting to the microphone.

SHELLY (*sings*): So you wanna be a rock'n'roll star
Then, listen now to what I say:
Just get yourself an electric guitar
And take some time
And learn how to play
And when your hair's gone right
And your pants are tight
It's gonna be all right!
Then it's time to go down town
To the agent man; he won't let you down
Sell your soul to the company
They're all waiting there to sell plastic wares
And in a week or two
If you make the charts
The fans'll tear you apart
What you give for your riches and fame,
It's all a vicious game
You're a little insane

All you get is the public acclaim
Don't forget who you are
You're a rock'n'roll star, la la la la la la la
la la
Hey you, come here, get up
This is the area where everyone creates
Recognise my face!
They blow me pumping gas
That's because of the sound that I get
My head's unlet
Once you've paid for all this vicious fame
Well it's all a vicious game
You're a little insane
For the things that you gain
Because of the public acclaim
Don't forget who you are
You're a rock'n'roll star.

Drum solo on fade out of the number.
SHELLY takes a bottle of champagne
during this loud finale: explosion of booze
and she swigs from the bottle. Then red
light. She gives a roadie the bottle and
returns to the microphone.

If it's love that you want
Baby, I've got it
From the depth of my soul
Baby you've got it
But I've been watching you
And I don't think that's your game
I tell you, there's no need to explain
Anyway that you want me
Anyway that you take me
Anyway that you make me feel part of
you
Anyway at all.
There's dreams in your heart
And dreams can last forever
From the depth of my soul I'll make them
come true
But I've been watching you
And I don't think that's your game
Come on in there's no need to explain
Anyway that you want me – etc.

She exits as band plays instrumental finale
of this ballad.
Blackout.

Act Two

June 1979.
Silence. Sound of cutlery. Lights up.
MAX *and* JOYCE *are laying the table.*
A large room of the big country house.
Enter SHELLY, *in a jacket and old jeans.*
She slowly walks round the table inspecting
it.

JOYCE: If you'll excuse me.

MAX *and* SHELLY *both watch her*
slowly go out.

SHELLY: She doesn't say much.

MAX: Mrs . . . my wife, she's on the reticent
side.

SHELLY: She talks to everyone in the
village.

MAX: Ah –

SHELLY: They natter for hours. I've seen
them.

MAX: She's known them a long time; many
years.

SHELLY: She doesn't even say hello to me.
She just nods. Like she's trying to get
some pigeon shit out the rim of her hat.

Pause.

She doesn't like me, does she?

MAX: I don't think . . . that's the case at all.

SHELLY: This is my house. My estate. My
land.

MAX: Dinner . . . Do you know how many
are coming?

SHELLY *ignores him. She paces.*

SHELLY: They're unreliable. It's the
hottest June since . . . '76? There'll be
quite a few. For dinner.

MAX: An approximation? And when?
What time should –

SHELLY: We don't work to timetables,
you know.

Pause.

MAX: I wonder if I might ask something,
Madam?

SHELLY: Madam? Oh – me! Go on.

MAX: My wife and I, we're having difficulty
sleeping. At night.

SHELLY: So hot.

MAX: Not the heat at all –

Pause.

SHELLY: Want some Mandies?

MAX: Pardon?

SHELLY: Sleeping pills? To sleep.
Mandrax: that beautiful woozy feeling.
They blurr the edges.

MAX: We don't partake. The reason is, we
can't sleep, if you'll forgive my
mentioning it – the reason is the noise.

SHELLY: Ah.

Pause.

MAX: We find it very difficult to sleep with
. . . all the noise. In the early hours.

SHELLY: We're trying some new numbers
– for the next album.

MAX: We can't . . . even get off.

SHELLY: We've got to get ready for the
album; it's in the contract.

MAX: Isn't it possible – to do it during the
day?

SHELLY: What's that?

Pause. SHELLY *wiggles a finger in her
ear: inspects wax.*

MAX: I was mentioning the possibility –

SHELLY: Yes?

MAX: Of your working during the day.

SHELLY (*incredulous*): What?

MAX: As opposed to all night. Night after
night.

SHELLY: I always work at night. I sleep
during the day.

MAX: And we . . . work during the day.
And sleep at night. Like the vast majority
of people in the world.

Pause.

Madam.

SHELLY: What do you do?

MAX: Do?

SHELLY: Your work? She cooks and
cleans and dusts. You –

MAX: It's an old house and a large house.
I'm always occupied.

*They stare at each other. Then SHELLY
inspects the table again, touching
crockery.*

SHELLY: How old is this . . . stuff?

MAX: It has been in the house centuries.
It's very fine.

SHELLY: Is it worth a lot?

MAX: I would hazard . . yes. A very great
deal.

SHELLY: How much?

MAX: I don't know the prices.

SHELLY: Take it away.

MAX: Pardon?

SHELLY: Don't leave it here. The people
coming – they're in the habit of nicking
knives and forks. Breaking plates. They
treat everywhere they eat as though
they're in a freeway diner.

MAX: Surely –

SHELLY: They're compulsive plate
smashers and cutlery stealers. Habit, you
see. The price of hotel living. Shall we do
a swop?

MAX: I don't understand what you mean?

SHELLY: You and your missus – bring
your knives and forks and plates in here
and you can have this lot.

MAX: It must be worth perhaps . . . I don't
know . . '. several thousand pounds.
More.

SHELLY: Yours. Swop. Yes?

MAX: Are you sure? Temporarily, of
course. They're almost irreplacable.

SHELLY: They'll only be nicked and
smashed. Otherwise, I'll have to get
plastic knives and forks and paper plates.
Might as well take the stuff, you know. Or
we'll have nothing left here.

MAX: Might I ask, who are these people?

SHELLY: They're musicians. Rock 'n' roll.

MAX: Ah, 'your' people –

SHELLY: 'My' people, yes.

MAX: I didn't mean to imply –

SHELLY: I know what you meant.

Pause.

There's going to be changes in the sort of people who come here. The guests. I noticed the guest bedrooms' beds –

MAX: They've been aired.

SHELLY: I want water beds. Every room. Don't look like that. Listen: The old man who ran this place, he isn't here anymore –

MAX: He was a very popular man, with everyone, in the village. Here.

SHELLY: They had to call the Official Receiver in. Bankruptcy court. Villain. I bet he wasn't so popular then. Hand in the till. Tut, tut. Oh dear.

MAX: Even after that . . . unfortunate . . . when the estate was on the market, madam – he still held the village firework night party here in the gardens. As he had done for twenty years. And everybody came. He was a fine man.

Pause.

SHELLY: You're very loyal to him.

MAX: I was with him . . . a long time. Since the army, the war. I served him from 1940 –

SHELLY: You must be loyal to me now, Max. I'm your new master.

Pause.

MAX: Perhaps you'll give thought to the noise at night.

SHELLY: We'll have a proper studio built in the stables.

MAX: What about the cars?

SHELLY: Leave them in the yard. That'll do.

MAX: They'll . . . go rusty. Do you really need all of them?

SHELLY: Tell her; ten for dinner.

MAX: Very good. And . . . about what time?

SHELLY: Whenever they get here.

MAX: When might that be?

SHELLY: Listen – we're not planning the Battle of Britain, you know. We don't have to synchronise watches.

She's looking up at the minstrel's gallery. MAX goes to her, points at it.

MAX: When Mr Richardson had . . . occasions here, sometimes a quintet would play up there, for his guests. It was very pleasant.

SHELLY: What did they play?

MAX: Waltzes. To dance to.

SHELLY: And danced down here?

MAX: Yes.

SHELLY: What about his daughter?

MAX: He had three. The youngest one – she liked your sort of music, madam. In fact, on her twenty-first birthday the garden was given over to her party. They had a marquee beside the orchard. There was a pop group playing. The trees were in blossom. The lake had swans then. The scent of cherry blossom.

SHELLY: Really? Yeah . . .

MAX: Shall I remove the cutlery then? And the plates.

SHELLY: Just the plates.

MAX begins to do this.

I've . . . never owned a house before. Only rented apartments.

MAX nods. He collects the plates. She goes behind the tapestry to climb the staircase. HOWARD enters. MAX doesn't see him. HOWARD looks around. SHELLY leans over the minstrel's gallery. HOWARD points, laughs, shouts.

HOWARD: Lot of fucking mud. Mud, mud, mud. In June!

He takes a knife to wipe the mud from his boots.

SHELLY: There's a thing to wipe it on. In the hall. Somewhere.

HOWARD: All this wetness, fantastic mushrooms, you could raise here, you know. You could grow 'em by the river, very pure, you know. Only thing is, how the fuck will you know if they're poisonous or not? That's the thing with mushrooms, as I understand it. There was this chick, in Wales. Few years back now.

SHELLY laughs; MAX continues his work, uncomfortably. HOWARD lights up a joint: an 8 skinner.

She had this cottage thing, got it, for the

mushrooms. That's what she bought it for. Her old man was loaded. He bought her this cottage. Get her outa the way. She'd got heavily into acid at Benenden. It took hours to find; the weekend I went there. Pissing down. We fucked a lot and picked the mushrooms and enjoyed the mushrooms and fucked – the whole weekend. So cold she kept her wellies and duffle coat on all the time. It was like fucking Captain Ahab. And when I got on the train home . . . then I realised it had been her period, like. The weekend, she was on, heavy, like. There was all this cunt blood. All over my face.

MAX *staggers, breaking a wine glass. They look at him.*

MAX: I seem to have everything . . .

SHELLY: Really Howard. Moderate your anecdotes when servants are present.

Without looking at them MAX *begins to go.*

HOWARD (*to* MAX): Hey, you know about mushrooms – how to grow them here?

MAX *goes out with the tray of crockery.*

It's great here Shelly. A butler?

She comes down.

SHELLY: Comes with the house. Do you think he remembers me?

HOWARD: How should I know?

She kisses him. Looks at his eyes.

SHELLY: Glad you came. You are a fucking pill head.

HOWARD: You know, I *need* it. I never thought I needed it. I just thought I needed it for playing. I can't get outa bed without it now.

SHELLY: Oh, well – better than painkillers.

HOWARD: Yeah. DFs . . .

SHELLY: All this . . . pain (*Pause.*) You know; no-one in England took downers until they introduced decimalisation. It's a fact. My accountant's fraud advisor told me.

HOWARD: Where's everyone else?

SHELLY: Not here yet.

HOWARD: What's that – a minstrel's gallery then?

SHELLY: High. They say, you don't get depressed. You don't get depressed if you're high . . . if you can look down. If you can get . . . high enough up you don't need drugs at all. Where's Sandy?

HOWARD: Ah, she couldn't come.

SHELLY: I wanted everyone to bring their wives.

HOWARD: She's . . . you know . . . And the journey. All this way. We're having a lot of trouble with babysitters.

SHELLY *coming down stairs.*

SHELLY: Well. I dunno. I never thought I'd live to see the day a guy in a fast, fast rock 'n' roll band said fucking baby sitters were messing up his social life and . . . (*Pause.*) The au pair –

HOWARD: Gone back to Thailand. This'll be cold in winter.

SHELLY: This is a house for social things. We could have had a barbeque in the orchard or something tonight –

HOWARD: Can I help myself to a drink then?

Takes one of the many wine bottles on the table.

SHELLY: There's a wine cellar. Here. I went through it last night.

HOWARD: Good stuff?

SHELLY: I couldn't find a bottle opener . . . thousands of bottles. (*Laughs.*) I got Jimmy to fit up a system up there –

HOWARD (*pouring drink*): Yeah?

SHELLY: I want to work up there. All the equipment I need; up there, Jimmy did it. The sound's good. Listen.

She goes up as STEVE *and* RICKY *enter; she is a grinning blonde.* SHELLY *is setting up a tape.*

STEVE: You made it. Sandy?

HOWARD: She couldn't –

SHELLY: You're here?

STEVE: Yeah. This is like the Elizabethan motel in Alabama. It's fantastic.

HOWARD: Fawlty Towers. You have to

pour your own drinks –

STEVE: How much did this cost?

HOWARD: Costs a fortune in gas just coming up the drive.

STEVE: Filling station at the gates?

SHELLY: What, in a stately home?

She laughs, Sibelius No.2 floods out as she comes down.

STEVE: What's that then?

SHELLY: Sibelius. I was . . . hum . . . playing it, you know. Have a drink.

STEVE: This is Ricky.

SHELLY: Oh.

STEVE: I brought her.

SHELLY: I see.

STEVE: Here.

RICKY: Hello.

Pause.

SHELLY: Hello.

RICKY: I admire very much your songs and I like especially 'Here Comes the Night,' and I very much admire you when I see you in the flesh.

SHELLY (*coming down*): Shall we get all these compliments outa the way then? I bet you . . . are . . . terrific in the flesh.

RICKY: Thank you so much.

SHELLY: Steve, you have . . . taste. Your taste buds are – is she succulent?

RICKY: Thank you so much. I see you Shelly first when I am student and you come to Copenhagen.

SHELLY: Danish?

RICKY: No, I am from Amsterdam.

SHELLY: I like Amsterdam. I like it a lot. My favourite city. When did you leave?

RICKY: When I am fourteen.

SHELLY: To leave Amsterdam. Where did you live?

RICKY: You know the Bilderdijkkade?

SHELLY: No.

RICKY: I have a friend there who says he knows you good. He fucked you two times in the Frascati. On the bar.

Everyone is watching you.

SHELLY: Not me. My double. She pretends she is me. In Amsterdam I only know the American Hotel.

RICKY: That's not real Amsterdam.

SHELLY: They're *real* tours. They're designed to make everywhere feel the same. So we don't get homesick.

RICKY: Often I see you on T.V. when it is shown in my country.

SHELLY: I could come to like Sibelius. H trained as a lawyer you know. Good training for this business. I'll turn it off.

She goes up and turns it off as:

HOWARD: Recording any of the stuff you've been writing?

SHELLY: Nar, it's not for us. It's no good for us. It's not rock 'n' roll.

HOWARD: Who's it for then?

Pause.

SHELLY: I dunno.

Music goes off. Pause.

STEVE: How's Sandy then?

HOWARD: I haven't asked her lately. All right I think. Yeah, she's not complaining.

STEVE: Is Caryl coming?

SHELLY: I hope not. I never asked her.

STEVE: I went into the office today. She's all over the place.

SHELLY *comes down from the gallery.*

SHELLY: I don't know what to do about her. She's . . . so unreliable. She's supposed to be *my* personal assistant. I can't cope with her problems. I have to solve them before she can reliably write down mine.

STEVE: She's . . . always snorting.

SHELLY: I was fucking annoyed about Berlin.

HOWARD: Be fair, had Bill really got the dates?

SHELLY: Of course he had. And Caryl . . . shit . . . she never even replied to the promoter's letter. I spoke to him myself on the phone after the Kraut journalists came on about us pulling out, for fuck's sake.

STEVE: She said his letter arrived late.

SHELLY: All I'm saying is –

HOWARD: But did Bill go to Berlin when he said –

SHELLY: I WANTED BERLIN BADLY. And . . . Caryl . . SHE BLEW IT.

SHELLY *sits at the head of the table. Pause. Then she pours drinks for all. HOWARD and STEVE use silver trays to arrange lines of cocaine. A joint is passed around.*

SHELLY: She says it'll be airtight for December. The new tour.

HOWARD: You want to tour Europe again before –

SHELLY: Why not?

HOWARD: Well, I –

SHELLY: I'm not a hermit, you know. I'm not a recluse.

HOWARD: Right.

SHELLY: Three nights in Berlin, the promoter said. He saw what we did in Kassel and Munich. He's hot for us. I dunno whether to sack Caryl.

She hands round drinks. The cocaine and the joints are passed round the table too.

HOWARD: She has been with us a long time.

SHELLY: Maybe, too long. It's not the Civil Service, you know.

STEVE: She didn't take coke at all until she came with us to L.A.

SHELLY: So? I think I'll ask Bill to sack her.

RICKY: I know typing very good.

STEVE: You're with me.

SHELLY (*passing joint to* RICKY): I'm not here much.

Enter ALUN in black gear. He wiggles his arse and sings in a Rod Stewart voice.

ALUN: Do . . . you think . . . I'm sexy . . . do you think I'm a pouf?
I've bleached my hair and donned falsies
I've a beauty spot on my cheek
Do you reckon we could make our ends meet?
Hello, I'm Alun. (*This to* RICKY.)

STEVE: I dunno why he talks in that fucking Scotch voice.

SHELLY: Berlin'll be better in December.

ALUN: So we're doing it again?

SHELLY: Last three nights of the tour. After Amsterdam. To finish.

RICKY: Where in Amsterdam?

SHELLY: Carré. The old circus.

RICKY: Oh, so big.

SHELLY: The guy from the Melody Maker was fascinated we're so big in Iceland.

HOWARD: You did the interview after all?

SHELLY: I forgot he was coming, so I had to see him.

HOWARD: How did it go?

SHELLY: He was boring. He just kept asking questions. A lot of journalists are like that.

HOWARD: About the new album – did he ask anything about how it'd be?

SHELLY: You know, he liked the last single. Wish he'd done the review. I think people who like me are more boring than the people who hate us.

HOWARD: But it went well?

SHELLY: I'm getting a lot of wax in my ears, you know. I bought a magnifying screen for the T.V.

RICKY: I see you at Carré once.

STEVE: Ricky, leave it out. Have another drink.

ALUN: I got some great videos. This guy from the Vice Squad . . . Later, yeah? –

SHELLY: None with animals though. They make me sick. Now I've got animals around me. Here.

ALUN: You'll never remember to feed them. They'll all die.

They laugh.
TREV *enters. He mimes Richard III.*

TREV: If you don't let me into this . . . fucking hotel . . . I'll stuff me whole hand down me fucking throat and make meself sick and vomit bile and spew and mouth shit all over your customers.

He stuffs his hand down his throat and makes a choking noise. Everyone laughs.

So . . . Fawlty Towers then . . . this is all right. I mean, this has the size and style of a monstrous tax dodge. Home sweet tax evasion – (*Laughs.*) Listen – him, you know he's gone hunchback now . . . (*Sings.*)

Mister Big, you're a fascist pig. Your mother never told you, but I just did.

He wrote it. Dedicated it for the Prime Minister. Thatcher. Fucking called it Mister Big, You're a Fascist Pig. Recorded it. Then found out – she's a woman.

STEVE: You're joking?

TREV: Or some other reason. It's been , held up a week. So the tour's been put back so I'm not working so – I'm here. Who do you have to suck off for a drink?

SHELLY: Help yourself.

TREV: Don't tempt me Shelly. Torment. I'm still mad about you.

TREV *kneels and chews at* SHELLY's *arse. Laughter.* RICKY *gets on her knees to join in.* STEVE *tugs her off. Laughter.* TREV *pours a drink. He takes snort of two lines from a silver tray.*

How old is this place then?

SHELLY: Five hundred years, I think they said. It's in a book, something about it. It's called an estate, not a house.

STEVE: An estate agent sold it. (*Laughs. Silence.*)

TREV: Whatsit manor. In Essex. In England. In . . . the green fields of England. In the night. In a hot mid-summer night. A house built for a king and his whores. Bought by a rock 'n' roll whore . . . good on you Angel.

This like a toast. Silence.

RICKY: Where did your band get such a name?

STEVE: What – the Angels?

RICKY: Why that name?

ALUN: We won it in a cornflake competition. First prize was a British Leyland car. So we did fucking well.

RICKY: Don't you like it?

SHELLY: I hate it.

RICKY: Why?

SHELLY: If you can think of a good name, tell me. And we'll change it.

RICKY: After so many years?

SHELLY: Not *so* many.

RICKY: Sixteen –

SHELLY: When the lights are red on stage and I leap around, people think I'm still . . . seventeen. I . . . I'm not as old as *him*.

She shakes a champagne bottle and splashes TREV. *He laughs.*

TREV: My age is my . . . secret. I got it wrong –

SHELLY: I kept buying the paper –

TREV: See, News of the World . . . when they said forty – well, that was the name of his daughter. I mean the ambassador. He was called Forte. FORTE. His daughter, that was her name. Not my age – her name. Fucking John Cleese geezer, the ambassador.

SHELLY: All over two pages. I liked her picture. I . . . thought, yeah, I see Trev up that.

TREV: Angie, she was so mad. Cow from the hairdresser's brought it round on the Sunday afternoon. She sobbed. She said: 'My mum reads this paper and what's she going to say?' I said – 'Sod her, my mum reads this paper –'

STEVE: And what did *she* say?

TREV: She said: 'That's sure fucked your chances of a knighthood, son.'

Laughter.

Who wants a taster? The last of the San Francisco dust?

RICKY: Maybe you jump out of window?

SHELLY: What's that? You on acid? In Amsterdam?

RICKY: I live Copenhagen now.

SHELLY: I can't imagine anyone leaving Amsterdam. I can't imagine anyone leaving Paris, or New York or . . . Berlin . . . I even like Australia. I can't figure why anyone stays here. In this cess pit. In

England.

RICKY: You stay?

SHELLY: I'm . . . (*Laughs.*) I'm an artist . . . I need my native fix. I gotta have something to hate or I can't go on. And all this in England – I'll go on forever. No rock 'n' roll suicide.

ALUN (*to* RICKY): They say I'm sexier than –

STEVE: She's – with me.

ALUN: Why did you come here then? (*Still to* RICKY.)

RICKY: For my studies, I wish to come to reside for a year or two in London. I wait for opportunity to come to position for study in London. And then it comes.

SHELLY: Whereabouts?

RICKY: In Luton.

They laugh madly. Geeing RICKY *up. The joints are passed (already rolled in a cigar box).*

SHELLY: What are you studying?

RICKY: Customs. The customs of alien countries.

SHELLY: Oh well, that should definitely take a year or two, here. Or a night with me in my bed? OK?

MAX *comes in.*

Good evening Max. Don't worry about knocking before –

MAX: The door wasn't closed. Is everyone here now? I mean, may the meal be served?

SHELLY: Served. Served? S-e-r-v-e-d? We're not all here yet. People are coming from all over the . . . Home Counties.

MAX: I see.

SHELLY: This young Dutch lady from Copenhagen resides in Luton. She is very interested in our customs.

MAX: Good evening. I trust you are finding your stay here to your satisfaction.

STEVE *makes wanking signs.*

RICKY: Thank you, I am so –

SHELLY: Max, you are so . . . civil to foreigners. And so civil to English people who you think are . . . better than you.

I've seen that: Lords and Ladies, your knees shuddering beneath your balls; middle classes who flick snot at you, all genuflecting. Even foreign tarts like her. But to people you think are lower than you . . . he's nasty to us. He is nice to Ricky and Major Claughton and the Vicar and the debs' delights and . . . nasty to me. (*Pause.*) Would you like a toot?

She offers a straw.

MAX: I don't smoke. I'll see about delaying dinner.

MAX *goes.*

SHELLY: Ricky, you may discover – there are some quite . . . unpleasant customs in England. (*Turns to* RICKY.) Do you think Debbie Harry is a potential running mate for Ted Kennedy?

RICKY: I see her in Copenhagen when I am a student . . . you know . . . I like you better.

SHELLY: That's English, baby. Keep a civil tongue in someone's arsehole.

STEVE: You got women here then Shelly?

SHELLY *snorts again.*

HOWARD: Where's your dentist bloke?

SHELLY: He wasn't a dentist. He was an Australian gynaecologist. He got bored with it. So I'm all alone. (*Laughs. Sniffs. Breathes in deeply. Sighs.*) You know what a recluse I am. (*Laughs.*) I want to be alone – it was in the Daily Mirror. (*Laughs.*) All alone in huge country 'estate' somewhere in the green fields of Southern England. Hard to get hold of. Impossible to locate. (*Laughs.*) Nice bloke. Kid. Drink and chat. (*Laughs.*) Daily Mirror reporter – he wanted to fuck me, you know. (*Laughs.*) Said I'm hard to locate. I showed him the burglar alarms. The ansaphone. The ex-directory numbers. And if you can get through all that, you get Caryl, and since she's Caryl – no-one ever gets through to me, you know. They've ghosts here – men who came to read the meters and got lost and died wandering the east wing. (*Laughs.*) I never hear the phones in time . . . when I get to them they've stopped . . . I wonder what it'd be like, to be here alone. No-one else living here? The house . . . empty. In the winter. When it's iced up. Cut off. I wonder . . . if you'd go mad alone here, then?

She wanders away from the others.

ALUN: My brother got done. Dressed up as an Arab to rob a jeweller in Burlington Arcade. He stank of Scotch.

TREV: Dutch courage.

RICKY: Beg pardon. What is so funny?

TREV: I think they've voted me out.

Pause. They turn to distressed TREV. SHELLY *sits again, concerned.*

Sorry . . . sorry . . . I don't want to fuck the evening. Just –

HOWARD: What?

TREV: They've kicked me out.

SHELLY: Out of the band?

TREV: Yeah.

SHELLY: With an American tour next week?

TREV: Crazy. Ed's a crazy cunt – typical Ed, a stunt like this.

SHELLY: Who are they replacing you with?

TREV: I dunno.

HOWARD: But – it's crazy.

TREV: Have you heard the rumour?

ALUN: No – real shock. Not a whisper.

TREV: Then . . . maybe it isn't true. I just had a feeling he might have.

STEVE: You haven't been voted out?

TREV: You'd have been the first to hear if I had. I just . . . got a feeling they might. Not want me.

SHELLY: Did Ed say that then?

TREV: No, no, I didn't get this from Ed. In fact, no one's saying nothing. They're just carrying on rehearsing like nothing's going on. Matier than ever. That's what's made me suspicious. Something's going on.

ALUN: So, no-one's said nothing to you?.

TREV: No.

ALUN: No whispers?

TREV: Have you heard any?

ALUN: No. Have you?

TREV: No.

SHELLY: Fucking hell!

ALUN: Jesus.

SHELLY: You're gonna have to take something for your paranoia, Trev. Otherwise you'll start hiring private detectives to follow yourself and bug your phone.

TREV: They'll start colliding into the ones my wife hires.

SHELLY: It's all the fucking speed you take. Jesus – it's worse than smack.

TREV: It's fucking cheaper than smack.

SHELLY: It burns up reserves of energy. And you'll end up without none at all.

TREV: All that energy. No-where to go. Until here. (*At window.*) So much energy. So much fucking hunger and hope. It began the night in this garden.

SHELLY: You didn't say you remembered . . .

TREV: Over there. By the pond. In that fucking huge marquee. And them debs. Chinless fucking wonders. All risen without trace. Her coming-out ball. I felt so much older, so much wiser than them with their . . .

SHELLY: Ignorance.

ALUN: Ignorance?

SHELLY: Innocence?

ALUN: Innocent – them tarts?

SHELLY: The guys. Up there between the sets. The brother. Fucking Oxford blue, fucking something in the city. In the garage a Jensen Intercepter, and in the bedroom a premature ejaculator. I found the energy.

TREV: You *hated* them.

SHELLY: I work best on hate. (*Laughs.*) There was a lot of dope. Columbian Black.

TREV: A guy in Thatcher's . . . junior minister now. I saw him on T.V.

SHELLY: Being on T.V. is not the definite proof of existence. I've seen Britt Ekland on T.V.

ALUN: The first time we got a hundred quid.

SHELLY: Guineas!

TREV: Guineas! And the fucking van's clutch went.

SHELLY: We run out of petrol.

TREV: Oh, that's right!

SHELLY: And not a quid at the service station – not a quid between us. Just a fucking hundred guinea cheque! David had to pay.

TREV: He was the only one who had a job. Cash.

SHELLY: He had a very expensive wife.

TREV: Not now.

SHELLY: She's a fucking doctor, the new one.

TREV: Doctor is she?

SHELLY: A cunt!

ALUN: Ever see him?

SHELLY: My eyes are closed.

ALUN: The kids . . .

Pause.

SHELLY: Oh that . . . the first wife was a sex-shrink. With a parched womb. They got on famously. The wife and my babies. So she kept the kids. And my maintenance cheques.

ALUN: You pay – still?

SHELLY: I was the original liberated lady. I said: I'll pick up the tag.

STEVE: I showed her where you played. By the pond. In the garden. Lots of gnats by that pond.

SHELLY: I had hay fever.

RICKY: Such big gardens – orchard.

SHELLY: I was impressed by the size of it all.

RICKY: And now you own them.

Pause. They refill glasses. Joints pass again. They are slightly stoned now.

SHELLY: Yes.

ALUN: I said: 'Shelly, one day all this will be yours.'

TREV: David put his arm round your shoulder when the EMI guy offered –

ALUN: He smelt it –

SHELLY: What a stupid obsession.

TREV: Eh?

SHELLY: I wanted to buy *their* land.

TREV: The minute I thought: 'Hey. that lovely arse is going somewhere –'

SHELLY (*sings*): 'Where you lead, I will follow –'

TREV: I wish we'd had a fuck on that stage. It was very heady realising. Seeing it crystal clear. She was going to be a rock 'n' roll star.

SHELLY: I got so wet, I put knickers on for the second set.

HOWARD: You found out what to do here.

STEVE: Not the Marquee or Tiles?

HOWARD: Here!

SHELLY: I hated those fuckers.

HOWARD: First time you said it: Listen –

SHELLY: I've said that every gig for sixteen fucking years and no-one's ever written it down.

HOWARD: Listen, you arseholes. When the revolution comes you'll be the first to go. But in the meantime, let's have a good time.

ALUN *mimes and hums 'Here Comes the Night' intro.*
They all sing a bit. Drunken staggering laughter. In comes VAL *and* MIKE. VAL *is discernibly pregnant beneath a summer dress.*

MIKE: Not too late are we?

SHELLY: Any time you're here is a good time. Val, you look . . . great. Good to see you again.

SHELLY *kisses* VAL.

VAL: Mike played some of the new songs on the tape in the car coming down – they're . . . well, you know, don't you.

SHELLY: Great you came. You look – summery. All full of summer.

VAL: I wanted to see the place. Mike said it was . . . but . . . but, it's super.

SHELLY: Not a home though.

VAL: I'll swop!

MIKE (*about* TREV): What's he doing loose? I thought he'd have been arrested. National scandal, that. Even the News of the World was appalled.

TREV: I've heard in the States they're striking a special Congressional medal. Just me and John Wayne. One for him for fucking up the Indians and me for fucking the ambassador's daughter.

MIKE: You're touring the States again next week?

TREV: Including me?

SHELLY: His paranoia is very up front tonight.

VAL: The furniture – it's yours?

SHELLY: I bought the house and every-thing in it. It's . . . like a job lot. I even got the servants.

VAL: What about all your lovely stuff in London?

SHELLY: It was a lease. It ran out . . . this is . . . my new place. You see. I didn't want . . . those things anyway.

STEVE *pouring more champagne.*

VAL: Hello, my name's Val.

RICKY: Thank you, I like it very much.

STEVE: She's from Copenhagen. She's Dutch.

HOWARD: I GOT THE MUNCHIES!

TREV: Is this a gong?

HOWARD: Gong it and see.

TREV: Will the man come?

He strikes the gong, then plays a tune on it. They gather round gong. SHELLY and VAL are left alone. She fills her glass for her.

VAL: Are you here on your own?

SHELLY: Who else is there to be here?

VAL (*pause*): Cheers. So much . . . space. How many rooms?

SHELLY: Too many. It's . . . ridiculous. I realise it's ridiculous.

VAL: You mentioned your parents –

SHELLY: I don't think it'd . . . work out . . . them living here. I don't think they'd like

it. I sent them a photo of here.

VAL: How are they?

SHELLY: Oh, well . . . She has headaches. Me dad's quietened down a lot now he's retired. He's . . . quite different to how he used to be, when he was working. (*Drains her glass.*) I ought to go and see them soon.

VAL: And your siste‐ – how is she?

SHELLY: Oh, I talk to her on the phone. She's a total mum, you know. The kids. And a bigger house off the new estate. I wanted to get her a car – theirs's so unreliable, they never come here –

VAL: So, a car –

SHELLY: She wouldn't let me. I've got a Daimler and Mercedes rotting in the courtyard. She said they couldn't afford the petrol. (*Pause.*) She phones me up at the studio, keeps me in touch about mum. Her megrims . . . I ought to go and see them.

VAL: For a weekend?

SHELLY: Mum, you know – she still asks me about getting a 'proper' job, or getting married. Or I'll regret it in my old age. I'm sure she's right. I'm boring.

VAL: No you're not. And the guy in New York; what was his name?

SHELLY: Oh, him. Lost touch when we came back. He wasn't often in London anyway. He got depressed quite a lot. And I . . . I found that . . . err, depressing.

Crescendo on the gong. MAX *enters.*

TREV (*singing*): Why . . . why are we waiting?

MAX: You want me to serve now then?

SHELLY: You? No, what about Mrs . . . your wife?

MAX: She has retired for the night.

SHELLY: She's done . . . what?

MAX: She's . . . very tired.

SHELLY: Oh. Oh dear. I thought, you see, that she'd dish up.

Pause.

With you. Both of you.

MAX: She was taking advantage of the

quiet.

SHELLY: I pay you both wages. The two of you. This is the first time I've had guests, socially . . . the least you pair could do is –

MAX: Mr Richardson was always most understanding when –

SHELLY: I'm not Mr Richardson –

MAX: He never raised any objection to my alone doing the –

SHELLY: I want her here. Now.

MAX: But, she's asleep.

SHELLY: I want her serving . . . us.

TREV: She's the boss you know.

HOWARD: That's true. She's a capitalist landowner and she wears the trousers.

MAX: She's been asleep for twenty minutes!

SHELLY: Then you'd better wake her up.

MAX: This is the first night she's been able to get to sleep before three o'clock for a month and –

SHELLY: WAKE HER UP! I said.

VAL: Shelly, what's the matter with you? Surely –

SHELLY: She's so . . . rude to me. Rude.

VAL: Well, that's no reason to –

MAX: I shall serve them –

SHELLY: Oi, I said not just you. I said – get her up. Now.

MAX: This is intolerable – she's undressed.

SHELLY: That's no excuse. It's a very hot night, we don't mind people taking their clothes off – Ricky, take your clothes off, go on, get 'em off.

RICKY: You would like so much? (*She begins to undress.*)

VAL: Oh Shelly. Don't be so . . . stupid!

Pause. The band gather round, stifled laughs.

SHELLY: Is your wife really asleep?

MAX: It is quite late.

SHELLY: Then don't disturb her –

MAX: I'll get the dinner. Thank you madam –

MAX goes out.

SHELLY: I said, don't you disturb her. We'll wake the old fucker up instead.

She dashes to the stairs. We see her twiddle with the tape deck in the gallery.

VAL: Mike, what's all this about?

MIKE: I don't know.

VAL: Don't you?

MIKE: A joke, I guess. A laugh – or something.

TREV: Hey, there's no spare chicks here. Shelly, Shelly! Is there somewhere in this place where chicks go when they want to be fucked?

HOWARD: She's only been here a couple of months – maybe the butler'll know.

Loud rocks blares out: 'Sunspot Baby' by Bob Seeger. RICKY begins to dance. SHELLY dances with her; she helps RICKY out of her dress. Laughter. MAX comes in. He shouts but cannot be heard because of the level of the music. VAL switches the music off abruptly.

MAX (*shouting*) – given the class of person . . .

Silence.

SHELLY: What was that?

MAX: The noise . . . it was deafening.

TREV: Bob Seeger is huge in Detroit. He hasn't made . . . Saffron Walden.

MAX: My wife is trying to sleep.

SHELLY: I don't mind, after all. I told you – you serve up and let her sleep, as long as we get the food.

MAX: She can't sleep with the noise –

SHELLY: It's my house, you know. It's not hers.

VAL: I've switched the music off.

MAX: I'll . . . get the dinner.

He goes. Laughter. VAL comes down. ALUN is setting new lines of cocaine.

TREV: I meant to ask him where the hookers hang out here.

HOWARD: I bet he's at it all the time.

ALUN: It's where the phrase comes from. Prince Albert – Queen Victoria stuff, his

head between her legs and she says:
Albert, keep a stiff upper lip.

VAL: Shelly, this is a little childish, isn't it?

TREV: CHILDISH CHILDISH
CHILDISH. That's the trouble with you
Shelly – you're so . . . CHILDISH.

STEVE: Even her children remark how
childish she is.

SHELLY: My children . . . they're older
than me now.

VAL: Still haven't seen them?

SHELLY: Her lawyers. To have access to
them I need to be fucking superman. I
wrote them, asked them down, if they
chose . . . to come here. If she let them . . .
them . . . the children she had from me.
(*Pause.*) Ricky fancies Max!

RICKY: Who is this Max, if you please?

TREV: Steve, you ain't upset –

HOWARD: She's wetting herself for Max.

STEVE: I know my place. I shan't
complain.

SHELLY: Then I shall have to severely
chastise Max. I can't have my staff
offending my guests by stealing their
women –

VAL: Shelly this is getting so –

ALL: CHILDISH.

MAX *comes in with food on a trolley.*

HOWARD: Dinner is now being served?

MAX: Are you eating sitting or standing –

*Pause. He puts the pot on the table. He is
about to go.*

SHELLY: Err Max, one moment –

MAX: Madam.

SHELLY: There's a . . . terrible smell.
Have you farted? (*She lifts the pot lid.*)
What is this?

MAX: Beef, madam.

SHELLY: It smells . . . disgusting. It smells
. . . vile.

MAX: I can assure you that the beef –

SHELLY: It's . . . got maggots in it. It's all
sweet and sticky and rotting. A terrible
smell. We can't eat this. Who . . . who
cooked this?

MAX: You're mistaken, I assure you –

SHELLY: WHO COOKED THIS?

Pause

MAX: You know perfectly well –

SHELLY: The cook was?

MAX: – perfectly well that there is –

SHELLY: I'm not risking poisoning my . . .
musicians. If I poisoned my musicians to
death, their union would black me.

MAX: As you like, then I shall remove the
offending –

SHELLY: Oi, arsehole. Stay. I said,
ordered, stay. This is an abortion. I'm
very displeased with you. The first time I
have a dinner party here and . . . you
humiliate me with this disgusting
concoction.

MAX: Goodnight, Ma'am.

SHELLY: Ricky, piss on him.

RICKY: I'm not understanding –

SHELLY: Hold him. Ricky. Get your
knickers off.

MAX: Please, unhandle me.

SHELLY: It's a citizen's arrest for trying to
murder us. My children's step-mother
could test the freshness of food. She has
this test. She throws it at people and if it
sticks to them –

*She hurls food at MAX and it slides from
his face. He is being held by TREV and
HOWARD.*

TREV: It fell off.

STEVE: Stupid bleeder. Wrong test. Eggs.

SHELLY: Oh, if the eggs floated they was
off. Sorry Max – I'll wipe it off. I did it
wrong. I apologise. The bloke who
fathered my bastards misinformed me
when providing character references with
regard to the proposed adoption. I was on
a lot of acid then. I got it wrong. It wipes
off.

*She wipes the food over his face and
jacket.*

VAL: Mike, I want to go home. Now.

MIKE: What, now?

VAL: Yes, now.

MIKE: Why?

VAL: Goodnight everyone – we're going home.

SHELLY: Val, you can't go – I wanted to talk to you.

VAL: Bye.

She goes out.

TREV: Val's going.

HOWARD: Val looks as if she's going.

SHELLY: She's . . . gone.

TREV: Even less chicks now. On this hot summer night in England.

HOWARD: Butler, where do we go to pull wide legged cock suckers?

MIKE: Shelly, I'm sorry – I don't know what's the matter with her.

SHELLY: You'd better drive her home, Mike.

MIKE: I'm sorry, you know –

SHELLY: Night, Mike.

MIKE: It's since she's been doing this Open University course, you see –

He goes. Pause. SHELLY watches their departure.

TREV: Tell me, my good fellow, when you fancy a vulgar fuck where do you go?

SHELLY: He'll have to cook something else. This food is . . . disgusting, disgusting – an insult.

She hurls it round the room.

MAX: I intend to go to bed now –

SHELLY: You don't. I'm dissatisfied with everything you've done.

MAX: Ma'am, if your intention is to arouse my –

ALUN: Ricky, he wants a bit –

HOWARD: It's an English custom.

RICKY: I student of customs.

TREV: Guests in posh English houses always fuck the servants. It's instead of leaving a vulgar tip. It's an unspoken sign of gratitude.

HOWARD: Jeeves, fuck her.

RICKY: This is strange English evening.

TREV: Shall I take her knickers off then?

SHELLY: No, I'll do that.

SHELLY *takes RICKY's knickers off. She laughs. MAX tries to free himself unsuccessfully from the men who hold him.*

SHELLY *touches RICKY: Pause. Everyone looks.*

I digress. (*Laughs.*) I must reprimand the staff.

HOWARD: Get him on the table –

They lift him onto the table. They hold him down.

HOWARD: Max, zipper down. Pants – off – now.

Laughter. MAX's trousers are removed. During this SHELLY goes up to the gallery. She looks down.

MAX: I object most strongly to –

SHELLY: You're a servant. You do as you're told.

MAX: Depending on the sort of person one –

SHELLY: Don't use that tone of voice to your master, Smithers. Not when you're stark bollock naked. If it doesn't offend the rules of country house etiquette it certainly contravenes my sense of what is permissibly absurd.

TREV: I'm sorry if you're offended Ricky – very rude a man turning down his cock when –

HOWARD: I don't know the class of servants you have to put up with nowadays –

TREV: He needs horse-whipping for his impertinance.

SHELLY: Can you ride, Smithers? Mount a filly in style?

MAX: Pigs . . . animals . . . ignorant . . . scum – scum – scum –

SHELLY: You shan't stop us with clever rhetoric like that, Jeeves.

MAX: In the morning –

SHELLY: In the morning, what?

MAX: I shall contact my solicitor.

SHELLY: I've got an army of 'em. Gobble yours up.

MAX: I shan't endure this –

SHELLY: Your old governor's in a debtors' prison, Smithers, with only his knighthood to keep him warm.

MAX: He is a fine man.

SHELLY: He's *so* loyal.

MAX: I served Mr Richardson since he was a captain in the Royal Artillery – years ago.

Derisive laughter.

He was a gentleman.

SHELLY: He wasn't a snob, Smithers. Not like you. Not a FUCKING SNOB LIKE YOU, Max. I met him. He was . . . charming. No side. No . . . snobbery. I met his daughter. At her birthday party. Here.

MAX: Here?

SHELLY: She was . . . all right. they were all all right . . . here . . . in this stately house. The only snobby bastard was you . . . the fucking servant. Rude, to us. Constantly offensive to . . . me.

Pause. They stare.

MAX: I have no recollection of –

SHELLY: I tell you, you were a frightful snobby shit, you know. I hate your snottiness. You are full of snot. Ricky, gobble out his snot.

RICKY: Hot von domer!

SHELLY: He is full of snot. Careful, it'll choke you. Spit it out in huge mouthfuls.

RICKY: I can't see it –

SHELLY: Keep still while Ricky inspects your prick Smithers. To attention.

RICKY: So small.

MAX: This is perverse –

SHELLY: No-one's fucking asking you. You . . . had your chance. Ricky, suck him off.

MAX *struggles. They hold him.* RICKY *begins to suck him off. Noise.*

JOYCE, *his wife, comes in in a dressing-gown and hairnet.*

Pause. They see her. RICKY *stops.*

JOYCE: Max, Max – what on earth is . . . happening?

MAX: Oh . . . Joyce.

JOYCE: What is . . . happening?

MAX: Joyce, they – I don't understand.

JOYCE: In all the years my husband has worked here, never has . . . this happened to him before.

Pause.

Max, are you all right?

MAX: Yes, in a manner of speaking.

They release him. He covers his penis with his hands. SHELLY *can't look.*

They didn't like the food, terribly.

Pause. Then the sudden loud sound of a train approaching and passing. Then silence.

TREV: A train?

JOYCE: The line runs at the bottom of the orchard.

SHELLY: Her first words . . . in front of me. In three weeks.

JOYCE: Come to bed, Max.

MAX: In the morning, we shall tender our resignations.

MAX *and* JOYCE *go. Silence.*

TREV: You've lost your staff.

SHELLY: 'My comfort still.' Well . . . no food now.

TREV: There must be somewhere here . . .

SHELLY: There's a pub in the village, they have a disco tonight. Colonel's daughters bored out of their minds with local wallys. I could use some action.

TREV: Bring them back here?

SHELLY: Why not?

HOWARD: Take the motors –

SHELLY: It'll take you ten minutes on foot – come back up through the orchard – see the lights of the house from there.

STEVE: Ricky, come on – put your dress back on.

RICKY: I'm feeling so relaxed you know.

STEVE: We're going to the pub.

TREV: In English pubs, even on a hot night –

STEVE: You have to wear clothes.

RICKY: Oh. You don't want me to go, Shelly?

Pause

SHELLY: I don't fancy you at all. I'm afraid. Sorry.

RICKY *puts on her dress.*

TREV: You coming?

SHELLY: You go. I'll wait . . . you know, I wish his wife hadn't come in. You know what I mean?

Pause. They all go. SHELLY *is alone in the gallery. She hears doors bang off. She switches on a tape. The backing track of 'Stand by me'. She dashes downstairs and off. Sound of bolts sliding across doors.* BILLY *comes in through the windows.* SHELLY *returns to the room, switching off the main light. Just the light from the gallery remains. She sees him.*

BILLY: Hello.

SHELLY: How did you get in?

BILLY: The window.

SHELLY: Supposed to be a sophisticated burglar alarm.

BILLY: The window was open . . . it's incredibly hot.

SHELLY: How did you get here?

BILLY: The train. I got off when it stopped at the lights at the orchard there. I didn't even have to walk from the station. (*Pause.*) This sounds . . . old.

SHELLY: Ben E. King is old. Nothing wrong in being old. If you wrote this.

BILLY: No words.

SHELLY: The backing track, laid down for –

BILLY: For what?

SHELLY: The words. Me to sing over it.

Pause.

BILLY: What are they?

SHELLY: What would the promoters say if I gave you a recital for nothing?

She locks the window

BILLY: You sing them alone? A new record?

SHELLY: When everybody's gone. I like to do the singing alone.

BILLY: Just you and the music. On tape?

SHELLY: On a loop. It replays automatically – I can . . . once I did it a hundred times before I got it right.

BILLY: What one was that?

SHELLY: The song you kept asking for at Brighton.

BILLY: I hadn't thought you'd heard me.

SHELLY: You were right at the front.

BILLY: I thought, you didn't hear.

SHELLY: I did. We don't do that one any more.

BILLY: I thought you noticed me. I thought you ignored me. You kept looking at me.

SHELLY: I just . . . thought you looked like you had space.

BILLY: Nice, here. Lot of space.

SHELLY: I didn't invite you. I need the space myself.

BILLY: I thought you invited me at Brighton, in the hotel room.

SHELLY: I was drunk that night.

BILLY: Is that why you fucked me?

SHELLY: Did I?

BILLY: I wrote everything . . . in my diary. Everything. You can read it. I wanted to see you again.

SHELLY: No-one's supposed to know I'm here. Tight security.

BILLY: No-one stopped me coming in –

SHELLY: I've just sacked the staff.

BILLY: Why?

SHELLY: They offended me.

BILLY: How?

SHELLY: Oh, I can't remember the details. It's surreal, so old a grudge. It's . . . I need treatment. (*Laughs.*) Like the garden?

BILLY: Huge. Miles. Acres.

SHELLY: Scores, I suppose.

BILLY: I read about it –

SHELLY: What?

BILLY: This was where . . . it began. I read EVERYTHING in print about you. I'm a fan. (*Shivers.*) I'm a bit nervous, now.

SHELLY: Shall I phone a Minicab to take you home?

BILLY: I don't want to go back there, tonight. I won't try to stay in the morning. I'll get the train. There's one at 9.35. Before you wake up. I came . . . specially to see you.

SHELLY: Oh.

BILLY: It was stuffy on the train. Crowded. People going to the coast for the weekend I suppose. Their weekend cottages. With children. I wanted to tell them I was coming to you. I would have liked them to know where I was going. I wanted them to notice me. I feel I should be . . . noticed. I feel different since I came into you. I smiled all through the journey from Liverpool Street. I just smiled ridiculously at everyone. I think they imagined I was mad.

Pause.

It's stopped, the music, I mean.

Silence.

I'd like to hear you sing the words. Please.

SHELLY: I err . . . (*Pause.*) I need to be alone to do it. (*Pause.*) The vocals see, without anyone. (*Pause.*) I can't function in front of other people. I have to do it myself. (*Pause.*) Look, it's late, you know . . . (*Pause.*) It was quite unpleasant what happened here, when she came. Here, it was . . . disturbing. So I *need* to work. It's a simple song. I don't want anyone here. (*Pause.*) What's your name?

BILLY: Billy.

He takes off his cowboy boots.

SHELLY: Oh, I see.

The tape starts again. It plays again during:

BILLY: No-one started it.

SHELLY: It's . . . automatic.

BILLY: The one you sang a hundred times?

SHELLY: In a little studio . . . near Tottenham Court road. They all went home. The security man locked me in. I switched most of the lights off. Just the earphones and the dark and the click of the machine. I'd got it right when they opened the studio for the cleaning ladies. They made me a cup of tea. I was . . . exhilarated. It was . . . dazzling sunshine outside. It was . . . dawn. It was our first one to do anything abroad. It went gold in a week in America.

Pause.

I felt, you know . . .

BILLY: I felt . . . after Brighton . . . well, I think I'm quite a bit . . . well . . . I think about you a lot . . . I err . . . I advertised for all your old fan club stuff . . . it cost a lot . . . I err . . . you're in my head. I want you. See?

SHELLY: I want to get this work done tonight, see.

A loud knocking on door off.

That's them. The musicians. Back.

More knocks. Shouts.

I've locked them out, you know. They can't get in.

Knocks. Shouts. Then, car doors bang and motors rev and go.

BILLY: Why lock them out?

SHELLY: I don't need them now. It's on tape. It's err . . . quite personal. Someone who used to be in the band wanted us to do this. Do this one. I need the dark. For this song. If you don't mind.

She switches the room lights out. She goes up to the gallery. Just one small light on her in the gallery. She puts on earphones.

BILLY: Won't they be annoyed?

SHELLY: They expect it of me. They're used to it. This might take quite a while, I'm afraid. Until maybe . . . tomorrow morning. They've gone now.

BILLY: Yes.

BILLY *lights a cigarette and sits on floor beneath* SHELLY. *The tape starts again.*

SHELLY (*sings*): When the night has come and the land is dark
And the moon is the only light we see
Then I won't be afraid, no I won't be afraid
Just as long as you stand by me.

Stand by me, stand by me
If the sky that we look upon
Should tumble and fall
And the mountains crumble to the sea
I won't cry, I won't cry, I won't shed a tear
Not so long as you stand by me
Stand by me, darlin' stand by me.

At the end of verse two lights slowly fade.
The tape plays on.
No light.
The tape plays on again in darkness.

Act Three

November 5th 1979
The garden. Night. Uniform white garden
chairs scattered everywhere.
The Guy Fawkes night party.
Lots of voices off: kids shouting, laughing.
Soundtrack of Tom and Jerry movie being
shown on a large screen in the garden
somewhere off.
MIKE *sits alone playing with computer toy.*
VAL *enters.*

VAL: She's thought of everything. I got the
kids down right in front of the screen.
They love the movie show.

MIKE: Hundreds here. Open house for –
hundreds.

CARYL *enters*

CARYL: The entire village – and people
from other villages. It wasn't advertised
or anything – just word of mouth.

VAL: They know it's not the previous
owner's firework party?

CARYL: He was declared bankrupt. Gone
a year. When did Guy Fawkes do it?
What year?

VAL: I don't know.

CARYL: She spent two grand on fireworks.
I wrote the cheque. This'll be like the
Silver Jubilee celebrations or something.

VAL: Where is she?

CARYL: Still in the house I guess.

MIKE: It's locked though –

CARYL: She didn't want people wandering
in and stealing her records. She said:
They can take the carpets and the
furniture but spare me the records.
Actually she's burning a lot. A lot of the
old furniture – on the bonfire. She's mad
at me for missing the press conference I
think.

MIKE: She handled it beautifully. She
cracked jokes. Old ones, but –

CARYL: The NME smashed us again. The
single – destruction.

VAL: They certainly destroyed the syntax.
Has she read it?

CARYL: You can only get the music papers
here if you order them and she hadn't
ordered them. But she knows.

VAL: What time does it start?

CARYL: When the movie show has finished – good idea that, eh? There's a buffet too – free. And champagne. She made the order; then had a nervous breakdown in case it might appear flash. Cancelled the order. And then sent a telegram cancelling the cancellation. What's she on?

MIKE: We nosed in the tent – the girls who do it are at the Rainbow, aren't they?

CARYL: You remember the Rainbow? (*Laughs.*) She's after the Rainbow before Europe. They think it's a practical joke.

VAL: Why?

CARYL: Read the NME baby. Read the NME. The little shit called it Oedipus Rock. She'll kill herself.

MIKE: It takes thirty seconds to get the taste for luxury. It takes a lifetime to get over it. Can she afford all this?

VAL: We're talking about her as though she's dead. I'd better get Pia out of the car.

VAL *goes off.*

CARYL: Are you happy with her?

MIKE: We're married.

CARYL: Do you think you're happy?

MIKE: What are *you* on, Caryl?

CARYL: I was asking. I take your touchiness to indicate –

MIKE: It's a *ridiculous* question.

CARYL: I know. I've got no rock'n'roll. Just eighty vitamin pills a day and a bottle of Tequila in my bed at night. I think the roadies sound stupid singing BeeGees falsetto; you should be banned from singing BeeGee songs if you weigh in at sixteen stone. They only started singing them now disco's dead. God, the lengths they go to to stay out of fashion. I think they ought to fuck me every now and again.

TREV *comes on.*

TREV: I queued up. I queued up. I thought it was the queue for a piss, but it turned out it was the sparkler queue. I got my sparkler.

Twinkle Twinkle little star. Tell me where the fuck you are? Where is she?

He lights the sparkler.

CARYL: I'll check. She can't figure out what to wear. She's been trying on costumes all day. A truck from Berman's.

TREV *hands* CARYL *the sparkler and she goes.*
He touches the computer toy. 'Foul' sound.

MIKE: Angie with you?

TREV: Yeah. With the kids in the movie show. I said I was coming here. She didn't believe me. I said I was bringing the kids. She didn't believe me. She said: you take the kids when you screw your woman. I said: only if they have budgies to strangle. So I brought her here to prove I was coming – and she's convinced more than ever I was going somewhere else.

MIKE *laughs and pours champagne in paper cups. They sit on garden chairs.*

TREV: She's getting very reticent. That's the word. Reticent. What's it mean?

MIKE: Don't say much.

TREV: That's her. With me, I mean. She talks to her mother on the phone for hours. I can never get through. She's always engaged. When I come back off the road she has hysterics 'cause I haven't phoned. Women do get hysterical, don't they. Men don't – get hysterical. That's why I love Shelly. She may be a schizophrenic egocentric, neurotic paranoia head-case but she ain't hysterical. She's a good bloke, Shelly is.

MIKE: Cheers.

TREV: It's all coming down, you know. The age of everything. In Germany they go in for their first O.D. at about thirteen. It's a Kraut epidemic. In the States kids have heart attacks when they're twelve. I think English women get the menopause at 24 nowadays. Every wife I've had does.

MIKE: Two.

TREV: Too many. I've had to sell the house in Chiswick just to pay off the first one. Does Val talk much?

MIKE: How do you mean?

TREV: Really talk . . . to you?

MIKE: She's studying sociology. Soon

she'll only listen if she gets paid to.

TREV: I think I'm in love.

Pause. MIKE *laughs.*

MIKE: What's the doctor giving you for it?

TREV: It's serious. I'm in love with Angie's mother. I married the wrong one. She's fifty-eight. She's ripe. She's a widow. She got drunk at her husband's funeral. Over the port she made an indecent suggestion which I then put down to grief. She always conspires to go up the stairs in front of me so I can see up her dress. She is incapable of giving me a cup of tea without rubbing her bosom against my nose. When I'm in the house her teeth chatter with sexual excitement. At night I can hear her teeth chattering in the bedroom. They make the glass rattle and the Steradent fizz. Angie knows there is something very electric between her mother and me. As soon as her mum's GP gets the certificate signed guaranteeing she won't have another menopause, I'll shack up with her. It's the ultimate. You can't get back at them by fucking their friends any more. It's gotta be their mothers. What's Val's mum like?

MIKE: You're a pervert. Mary Whitehouse is right about you.

TREV: I didn't used to be. Angie's mum looks like Mary Whitehouse. I'm heavily into plump old women. I hate young women.

(*Sings.*) Dirty old women, they sure get on my tits
Smelly old widows –
They always want a bit
I think dirty old cows should leave young lads alone
Put on their surgical knickers and stay at home.

I wrote that in Miami. Miami . . . I was inspired. Good B side.

MIKE: I thought Ed wrote them all.

TREV: He owns them all. Every B side he's got. Shelly and me are Gemini twins. I used to think we were like twins.

STEVE *comes on.*

STEVE: Oh, so here's where it's all happening. Where's Shelly?

TREV: Have you ever heard anyone call her Michelle?

STEVE: Angie's sitting in the Cadillac. In the drive.

TREV: Eh?

STEVE: She's sitting in your car. She says she wants to go home.

TREV: Well, let her fucking sit there.

STEVE: She said she can't get the roof up. She's cold.

TREV: Let her freeze. Honest to God, what's the matter with her?

STEVE: I dunno. Top up?

He has champagne too. He tops them up.

They're all waiting for her. Shelly's arrival.

TREV: She's a right arrogant ponce ain't she? Asks the entire population of Essex to a party and then don't turn up 'til everyone's half dead with exhaustion. She wears people out. She wore me out in America in '68. I never recovered. I've been dehydrated ever since. I'm a medical phenomenon.

MIKE: Did Ricky come?

STEVE: Yeah. Yeah, –

TREV: Still getting up her then?

STEVE: Yeah.

TREV: Well, that's consistency for you.

STEVE: I think she might have moved in. Her clothes keep piling up. The bathrooms full of her scent and stuff.

TREV: It's when it's full of boxes of Tampax you get worried.

STEVE: I want to bring her when we do Amsterdam.

MIKE: Don't let her mention it to the other wives, or they'll all want to come.

STEVE: I never did Amsterdam. This'll be the first time.

TREV: Then you definitely don't want to take her. It's like – no questions. Absolutely anything. I mean – it's like England was. In the . . .

Pause.

In the sixties. Christ, in January it'll be the eighties.

Pause.

I sound like my old man.

Pause.
VAL *comes in. She's breast-feeding baby.*

VAL: Hello, Steve.

STEVE: The baby then.

VAL: Haven't you seen him?

STEVE: No.

TREV: You look like a renegade from Glastonbury.

VAL: How's that?

TREV: It was full of beautiful women breast-feeding babies. I couldn't concentrate. Looking out at them . . . tits. In the abbey ruins, a sea of breasts like cobblestones. And the babies sucking. Drove the P.A. mad.

MIKE: She never got to Glastonbury.

VAL: I got lost on the way.

TREV: It was going to be the GREAT . . . COMMUNAL CUM.

VAL: And then everyone found out they'd been wanking so much, there was no cum left to come.

Pause

Laurel and Hardy cartoons now – I mean, when are the fireworks going to start?

MIKE: It'll be really cold soon. The kids'll be getting – tired, too tired.

TREV: Where have all the Indian summers gone . . . I had the roof off the car coming down.

STEVE: I know, Angie said. Bitterly. I think it's a fantastic motor.

They laugh. Chairs scattered about in a disorganised way.

TREV: Eight miles a gallon. Oh, Yanks sure know how to wind people up. Have you seen us, Val? Been to see us?

VAL: No.

TREV: You could analyse our appeal. Do a thesis on us.

VAL: Actually, I'm taking the degree quite seriously.

TREV: Everyone is so serious now. No-one left to drive Rolls Royces into the swimming pools anymore.

MIKE: No-one can afford them anymore. Shall I see if Sam's okay?

VAL: He's happy enough. Anxious for the fireworks.

TREV: Where have all the good times gone?

Silence.

CARYL *comes in.*

CARYL: People are getting a bit impatient. The booze is running out. Should I call her and get it started or what?

TREV: Just start. Sod her.

CARYL: She might – be furious if she's . . I think she wants to light the rockets herself.

TREV: Oh fuck her. Get her down then –

CARYL: I can't. I can't cope with . . . no smack and a bummer album and her moodies.

TREV: Don't get hysterical, Caryl.

CARYL: I'm not fucking hysterical – I'm just coping.

Pause.

TREV: Do you want a toot then?

CARYL: Not now; Pimm is here, you know.

TREV: Pimm?

CARYL: He came up to talk to me. Just suddenly there he was.

TREV: Oh Christ. Where is he?

CARYL: Wandering. Shelly will go insane if she . . . sees him.

Pause.

TREV: Ain't this cheerful. I thought he'd be dead by now. The stuff he's been jacking up.

CARYL: He's registered.

TREV: He'd buy anything . . . anything on offer.

CARYL: I can't deal with him.

MIKE: As long as we keep Pimm away from Shelly.

STEVE: Why?

MIKE: Pimm got sacked.

STEVE: Oh.

CARYL: He was crying. He sold the old red Fender.

Pause.

Sold that fucking Fender!

TREV: Been better if he'd died. Where was he?

CARYL: By the railway line. Looking down on the house from the orchard. Trying to see Shelly at the window.

A train passes. Noise. BILL *comes in.*

BILL: How the new gentry live. Well, this is . . . quite an occasion. Public spirited. Val.

VAL: Hello Bill. You don't mind?

BILL: Breast-feeding is a little passé they say. But go ahead.

VAL: I wouldn't do this in front of the vicar.

BILL: Forget the vicar, spare the rabbi. (*Laughs.*) Caryl. You've organised this so well.

CARYL: Bring your family, Bill?

BILL: They're in France still.

CARYL: Lucky old them.

BILL: I haven't seen Shelly yet.

CARYL: Trev's about to get her.

TREV: I am?

CARYL: Before everyone goes home. She's a bit . . . down about the reception the album got –

BILL: Well, she's an artist. Artists take things too much to heart. I think it'll do very well.

VAL: I think it's the best thing they've ever done.

BILL: Is that so, Val? I'm sure you're right. Trev, perhaps you'll tell Shelly I'm here. To see the fireworks. After all, that's why everyone came.

CARYL: A lot came to see her.

BILL: Then they mustn't be disappointed. Not after the way you treated the housekeepers. (*Pause.*) I could have got them out in a more civilised way. And avoided the publicity. And it would have

been cheaper. I want to speak to her.

Pause. He smiles.

Champagne in paper cups. That's . . . cute, I suppose.

He pours one for himself. He raises the glass in a toast.

Champagne for our real friends. Real pain for our sham friends.

TREV: I'll . . . get Shelly then. And Pimm – what about –

BILL: Pimm?

CARYL: I'll get him a car. Get him taken away. If I can find him.

BILL: Tell Shelly to hurry up. Some people are going home already. And the tart in the Cadillac is abusing them.

This is spat at TREV *who has almost gone.* CARYL *goes.*

I don't think it'll be a good idea to take the blonde on the tour Steve.

STEVE: Well, I err –

BILL: Not a sound idea. If you don't mind my saying so.

STEVE: It wasn't definite. I hadn't even –

BILL: I overheard. When you told Mike. And I think it won't look good. You're the youngest Angel. You're –

STEVE: What?

BILL: Our token gesture to youth, you understand. You're the available Angel. The rest are boring married men with children and alimony bankers' orders. You're a hook, you see. Shelly for the men and dykes. You for the chicks and gays, see.

VAL: Isn't it a bit old hat?

BILL: This is business, Val, if you'll excuse me.

VAL: If Steve –

BILL: I have my reasons.

VAL: It's not the sodding Monkees!

BILL: Let me make these sort of judgements, Val. For twenty years my judgement has prospered. I use the same bespoke tailor for the same style blue mohair suits I bought in '58 and the same judgements. Both are enduring. As all my artistes will testify.

Pause.

BILL: I'm glad we had this talk, Steve. I'm glad we see eye to eye on this.

He takes a green laser beam night light from his breast pocket and holds it towards the baby.

Babies love light. Here you are Val. Let it shine in the child's eyes. And make her happy.

VAL: Him.

VAL *takes the night light.* BILL *goes out.*

STEVE: Her parents are in Amsterdam. I can't stop her going to fucking Amsterdam.

VAL: No.

MIKE *enters.*

MIKE: They've started showing the Tom and Jerry cartoon again.

VAL: It's a balls-up then.

MIKE: Fucking Caryl –

TREV *comes on.*

TREV: The house is all in darkness. I shouted but –

There is a sudden explosion of fireworks in the sky. Rockets. Cheers: Oooos and Aaaahs. They watch. More rockets and bright colours, glow of fireworks and bonfire in the sky now. Happy sounds off. Explosions.

On bounds SHELLY *in a fluorescent ring-master-like costume: tail coat, bow tie and top hat. Blows toy tickler: hugs the bloke. Laughs.*

SHELLY: Everything's all right?

VAL: You sure stretch them out – wind them up. They were going home.

SHELLY: I like to see – how far I can go? You know. (*Laughs.*) It's great. It's fantastic. This is my Guy Fawkes' persona. The fluorescent rocker. I got it from Bill's tailor – I put acid in his chicken barley soup and he came up with this.

STEVE: Bill's here.

SHELLY: Bill? What's he doing here? I thought he was still in the villa, still in the Cannes villa I bought him?

VAL: He came when the temperature dropped. I don't know if it was a coincidence.

SHELLY: Bill's all right.

MIKE: You organised it really well.

SHELLY: Better than the firework night parties used to be here?

VAL: They can't have been more lavish.

MIKE: The vicar's come.

SHELLY: When I have a party, *everybod* comes. I wish we'd done a show, you know. A little concert. I wanna play, I really feel like . . . playing. I gotta lot of energy.

STEVE: I'd love to play.

MIKE: It's too late now.

SHELLY: Next summer, we'll do a conce here. In the gardens. For a charity or something.

CARYL *comes on.*

CARYL: We thought you'd . . . died or something.

SHELLY: Caryl, you make me so tense when you get tense. If you don't start taking downers I'll be a champagne alcoholic.

CARYL: I couldn't find you.

SHELLY: I've been busy. I've made a Gu I made a Guy. You want to see my Guy [You touch me and I'll let you touch m Guy.]

She laughs. She goes off then returns wi Guy covered in a blanket. Like a magicia she pulls away the blanket.
The Guy looks like BILL.

Well? Madame Tussauds, are you watching?

CARYL: Incredible likeness.

SHELLY: And the suit, you like the suit It's . . . out of line, it's wild. I stuffed th pants with rockets and a roman candle. When it's on the fire –

VAL: I don't think that's a good idea, wit Bill here.

SHELLY: Eh?

VAL: Bill's here.

SHELLY: He's got a sense of humour.

VAL: Has he?

SHELLY: Yeah. I've heard him laugh. Once.

MIKE: That was in 1971.

VAL: He wrote it down in his diary.

SHELLY: You think it's a bad idea then?

CARYL: Yes, Shelly. I do.

SHELLY: For Christ's sake – it's only a joke. I didn't know he was coming.

VAL: He's creepy. He probably came when he heard you'd made a Guy in his likeness –

SHELLY: O, don't be stupid – how's he know?

VAL: He knows . . . everything.

SHELLY: You make him sound like the KGB.

VAL: He is.

SHELLY: He's a manager, that's all. He works for *me,* you know – it's not like the other way round, you know.

VAL: Well, I'm just saying –

SHELLY: Don't bring me down. Not when I'm up.

CARYL: You got coke?

SHELLY: Caryl, it's possible to be happy without coke. It is possible. I'm just happy.

CARYL: Whatever turns you on. This champagne's gone flat.

CARYL *goes off.*

SHELLY: There's gallons . . . Come on, Steve, we'll go and put it on the fire then.

STEVE: O, well –

Pause.

SHELLY: What's the matter?

STEVE: Bill's here. You know, I think maybe like Val said.

SHELLY: You're serious. What is this, a black magic fucking coven or something? This is a joke not a witchcraft ceremony.

Pause. HOWARD *enters.*

HOWARD: Shelly, there you are.

SHELLY: Are you really Howard, or are you an effigy for sticking pins in?

HOWARD: Eh?

SHELLY: Panicking people are contagious.

HOWARD: What are you talking about?

SHELLY: This is supposed to be a happy occasion. Fun and all that. This is a very expensive celebration; this is the first expensive party I've thrown spontaneously after intense planning since . . . I got off Mandrax.

HOWARD: I just seen Pimm. Did you know Pimm's turned up?

Pause.

VAL: Great Howard – you sure know tact.

HOWARD: What's the matter?

VAL: Caryl's seen him. She's dealing with him.

HOWARD: I didn't think you knew –

SHELLY: I didn't. I had no idea.

VAL: Trev's gone to locate him; Caryl's fixing a car for him.

SHELLY: What's he . . . doing here?

HOWARD: He looks . . . terrible (*Pause.*) He looks like he's going to stay alive for about . . . one more week.

SHELLY: I wish I hadn't known about all this.

HOWARD: He said he's sold the red Fender, you know the one he –

SHELLY: Spare me the . . . pornography. O no, this is . . . terrible. I can't deal with this, you know. I could imagine him selling blood or his eyes. I could imagine him with no eyes in his head but . . . (*Pause.*) Where is he?

VAL: Up by the railway line.

SHELLY: Well, he'll have to go. I can't face this.

VAL: It's okay, Trev's gone to –

SHELLY: Look, I don't need all this. Another drug casualty, you know. It's incredibly boring, it's a cliché. You can't move without finding junkies wandering around looking for the dream on Haight-Ashbury. I seen them there, I don't want them *here.* It's not my problem. I never got him hooked. I just sacked him when he was.

VAL: No-one's accusing you of –

SHELLY: I HAD to sack him –

VAL: We know –

SHELLY: Or we'd all . . . DROWN.

VAL: Yes.

SHELLY: I want him . . . away . . . I want him . . . you gotta get him OFF MY LAND.

VAL: Trev's gone to –

SHELLY (to HOWARD): How was he . . . ?

HOWARD: He, err . . he looks like a ghost. He was wandering out of the orchard . . . some kids saw him. They screamed. He . . . looked . . . quite frightening, really. He was falling around . . . he fell over the projector lead. The movie stopped. When they made the connection again he was standing in front of the screen . . . all in . . . bleeding light. He was . . . um . . . crying.

Pause.

SHELLY: I really can't bear this.

HOWARD: I tried to get him out of the way. He was clinging to me, I mean, really clinging on. He couldn't focus. I had to tell him who I was. Fuck knows how he got there. He was . . . he's all bony . . . clinging to me.

SHELLY: The last time I checked, they said some fucking Franciscan nuns were supposed to be saving him. Instead of heroin, they was supposed to be fixing him with God and Jesus. I can't be held responsible for people. I'm not in that game at all, you know.

HOWARD: He asked where you were. He asked me to – like, I never said where – he . . .

SHELLY: Trev must get him out of here. He needs very serious treatment.

HOWARD: Yeah –

SHELLY: What did he want . . . me for?

HOWARD: Well –

SHELLY: He needs the best specialist treatment. Why do I pay taxes? Me, he said me?

HOWARD: He wants a job. If you'll have him back, for old times sake . . . in some job. Obviously, he's gone. I mean, his fingers to start with, everything. He don mean playing.

VAL: He'll be as good as a deaf musician.

SHELLY: Deaf men can play! In New Orleans I got smashed with a deaf alto sa black. He said he couldn't learn nothing new, but . . . he could feel if the ones he knew were coming out right. Feel the *'beautiful tones'*.

VAL: Bill must arrange something permanent.

SHELLY: Bill made . . . thousands out of Pimm.

Pause.

I'm asking please: Could someone do something about this MONSTER roaming like a disaster area on my estat Otherwise I shall leave the country on th first available plane, even if it's a DC10.

VAL: Shelly, cool it.

SHELLY: This is . . . too much.

VAL: Steve, try and find Bill –

STEVE: He's never here when you need him. I'm surprised he hasn't materialise like when I said to Mike about taking Ricky to Amsterdam –

SHELLY: Tell him I must be sheltered fro Pimm.

STEVE: Right.

SHELLY: I can't cope with that, not now. coped with that for eight years. I coped with that every hour for eight years and . . . I couldn't endure seeing him the last time I saw him and that was two years ago. I don't know how people start injecting things into themselves. Into their . . arteries. Needles. When me and Pimm were at school –

VAL: What?

SHELLY: He fainted having a T.B. jab. Just the sight of the . . . thing.

VAL: You're shivering.

She leans against VAL and hugs her.

Pause. SHELLY *is crying.*

SHELLY: Please . . . don't . . . let go again

VAL: I want to cry myself.

STEVE: Did Bill say he was going to the food tent?

VAL: I don't know. Try there – maybe Mike, he went to see that Sam was okay, not scared of the fireworks.

STEVE *goes hurriedly.* VAL *still hugs the trembling* SHELLY.

SHELLY: O Jesus. This is so unfair, you know. I stopped caring about him years ago . . . and I still fucking care. I mean, he's not my brother or nothing, not flesh and blood, I mean, I tried everything; when I had good news I never told him in case it upset him. I – tried all I could think of. I paid for cures and the day he came out . . .

VAL: Look! Don't blame yourself.

SHELLY: I don't know why it hurts me so much. He's on cloud nine when he gets it. I'm the one with chinks of glass rubbing in my veins. He hurt everyone who cared about him. He loved his kids but he even used them to smuggle the junk through customs when we went to Spain, you know. In their toys. In his kids' toys. A promoter went bankrupt because he – we lost a tour and . . . because of his fucking tragedy. And I refuse to let him start fucking me up again now I'm all sorted out and unconfused. I don't know what attracts me to men with a blatant weakness.

Pause.
HOWARD, *stoned, stands helplessly.* SHELLY *still hanging on to* VAL.

HOWARD: Is there someone, some organisation we could phone?

VAL: The Samaritans maybe –

SHELLY: They're hopeless. They just let you ramble on. When you phone the Samaritans they don't say anything to you. I had to do all the talking.

HOWARD: Maybe they'll know who – a phone?

VAL: In the house?

SHELLY: It's all locked up.

HOWARD: Surely, for a phone –

SHELLY: It takes HOURS to unlock it, the burglar alarms and –

VAL: And empty inside.

SHELLY: Like me. (*Grim laugh.*) O shit.

VAL: Ridiculous a house that size –

A car horn sounds off.

SHELLY: I can't help the problems of the world. I got plenty of my own, you know.

VAL: I didn't mean –

HOWARD: I'll try see if Bill, at the food tent – they were running out a while back.

SHELLY: Then the caterers have robbed me 'cause those bastards cost enough to –

HOWARD: I'll see anyway. (*He goes.*)

VAL *calms* SHELLY. *More fireworks and silver sprays of light behind them, silhouetting them.* TREV *comes on, pauses;* VAL *sees him and pulls away from* SHELLY *as* TREV *sits, not wanting to see them. Pause. When* SHELLY *sits: she takes some dubes.*

TREV: He's gone.

SHELLY: Really?

TREV: He isn't where Caryl said.

VAL: You looked all along the –

TREV: I looked, right along the railway line. Not a trace. Really, everyone's going now . . not many left . . . he's not here. Maybe the house –

VAL: We'd have heard the burglar alarms.

SHELLY: Maybe, he's . . . gone with . . . friends or something?

TREV: Yeah! Where's all the champagne then?

SHELLY: No-one must ever mention him again.

Pause. MIKE *enters. Another car horn off. He hands* SHELLY *a joint.*

MIKE: Val, Sam's dropped off and . . . I put him in the car. I think we ought to, you know.

TREV: Last crate afore ye go?

MIKE: Angie's rammed something over the horn. It's making an incredible din. And she's shouting her mouth off at everyone leaving – about . . . what she imagines happens on the tours. *Your* tours.

TREV: She must be a lesbian, a dyke or something. She has fantasies about Californian girls. With big breasts and no suntan marks. She keeps getting me to talk about them. It's the only way she can come now without a vibrator.

MIKE: Someone tried to get the roof up for her and she said they were stealing the car.

SHELLY: Val is the only sane wife any of you had.

MIKE: I could tell you things.

SHELLY: Don't spoil my delusions. I gotta have faith in something. Now Lennon's retired you know!

She laughs and swigs from the bottle.

MIKE: I think we ought to go, Val. It is . . . late and time we got back.

SHELLY: Garden to weed tomorrow? Car to wash?

MIKE: Golf, actually.

SHELLY: Did you hear *that*, Chuck Berry?

TREV: We haven't burned the Guy yet.

SHELLY: The more I care about people . . . the more they screw me up. I think it's totally unreasonable of God to behave in such a manner.

CARYL comes on: she's dabbing her nose.

CARYL: There you are Shelly. Bill's getting a bit, kinda – looking for you. He's anxious to speak to you.

VAL: We've been looking for him.

CARYL: He was in the vegetable garden.

VAL: We never found him.

SHELLY: In a blue mohair suit, midnight blue. Pimm wore suits. He was very strict, two-tone mohair mod. The first chisel toes in our school.

CARYL: Is that a mod suit then, Shelly? Is it strict mod?

SHELLY: I feel ridiculous now. Like wearing drag at a family funeral. A clown's nose at a wedding. (*Pause*.) It's the same men in mohair who run it now as when we started: the same few. Bill and the others. Like Royalty.

Pause.

CARYL: Bill came specially, he said – to see you and –

TREV: At least Pimm's gone.

CARYL: If you see Steve, tell him Ricky's stripping in the food tent.

VAL: Again?

SHELLY: That body has become more familiar than caterpillars in me lettuce bed. I need a stiff Calvados. I could do with a bottle of Calvados next time someone goes abroad again.

CARYL: There's a lot of half empty bottles of champagne. Flat Moet, does that rhyme?

SHELLY: You can make anything rhyme if you sing like Van Morrison. You can sing election manifestos and make them sound like sacred psalms.

TREV: Dirty bastards. Someone's stubbed a fag out in the fucking bottle.

CARYL: Not poisonous.

TREV: It does make them hard to light up again.

He giggles at this ridiculously.

MIKE: Val, it is very late and the kids –

SHELLY: You'd make someone a wonderful mother, Mike.

Pause. ALUN staggers on. He is very drunk.

ALUN: There's no fucking Guy. No fucking Guy. There should at least be a fucking Guy. I promised the Master of the Hound's daughter I'd light the Guy.

MIKE: There? (*Points to Guy.*)

ALUN: Jesus. It's so real. And . . . nothing in the pockets, not a dime – how do I know this isn't Bill? (*Kneels.*) Bill, please release me from my fifty year contract. I want to buy a digital watch and a rival manager says he'll buy one for me. (*He goes, taking the Guy.*)

MIKE: Well, it was a very nice night.

SHELLY: You've gone flabby, Mike. Flabby when you talk, when you play. Flab flab flab flab.

MIKE: Well, perhaps it's because I'm not resisting middle age. It doesn't terrify me I've settled for growing old gracefully.

He begins to go. VAL *goes to follow, hesitates, looks at* SHELLY *who catches her wrist.* SHELLY *says to her urgently:*

SHELLY: Are you and Mike . . . all right? Having problems?

MIKE *has gone.*

VAL: It's called being married a long time.

SHELLY: I tell my sister she's the happiest married person I know. I think of you quite a lot. Friend.

VAL: Are you going to be all right tonight? Will you sleep with someone?

SHELLY: I wish you could stay with me tonight.

VAL: Take care. Eh? Friend. Girlfriends – special, rare.

SHELLY: I didn't get where I am today letting suicidal junkies wreak havoc on my lawns. Listen, that other night here, in the summer – I'm sorry if I embarrassed you.

VAL: I hated you for being so cruel.

SHELLY: It got out of hand. They were paid terrific compensation.

VAL: For cruelty? I used to fancy you quite often, I'm afraid.

SHELLY: I paid the price of . . . it all, really. See the house – it's so lonely. Now they've gone.

VAL: You're alone too often.

SHELLY: Mainly when I'm with people. I would like to get warm on you.

VAL: I think I might come and see you one day. I will.

SHELLY (*shakes head*): Can you drive?

VAL (*slowly smiles*): Goodnight, friend.

She goes. SHELLY *looks at* CARYL *but she's rolling a joint;* TREV *staggers with a champagne bottle and falls.*

CARYL: Trev, be careful –

He crashes through the chairs to the ground.

You've got a long way to drive.

TREV: We'll stay here tonight.

SHELLY: Go home, go home. Fuck off.

TREV: I'll never marry another woman

who hasn't passed her driving test. And I mean that. They ought to teach them how to do it at school. In cookery classes.

CARYL: To wait on *men*? I don't wait on men and I get paid to do it. I'm a P.A. I'm not a substitute wife and mistress and coffee machine. Trev, shall I help you?

TREV: Caryl, you couldn't help a fart bubble out of the bath water. (*To* SHELLY.) You are menopausing Shelly, and only when you acknowledge that will you find peace and true happiness. *He staggers off.*

CARYL: Shelly, you and Val are like secret lovers. Isn't Mike jealous?

SHELLY: Caryl, how come you never hear the phone ringing when I phone you?

BILL *enters with snack on paper plate.*

BILL: I hope I can't smell dope.

CARYL: Need a new sinus spray, Bill?

BILL: Trev's wife is causing a disturbance in the car port.

SHELLY: Yeah, Trev's gone to make it worse.

BILL: She's reversed into the catering truck and they can't get the soup urns out. I don't know why people stay together when they're tearing each other apart.

SHELLY: They try to keep abreast of their neighbours' social activities.

SHELLY *puts her top hat back on.*

BILL: That smells good.

CARYL: It is. Try it?

BILL: No thank you. (*Laughs.*) Funny, a lawyer neighbour in France – telling me about one of his clients. Thought he had a perfect system for smuggling grass in – in boxes of cricket balls. But it was busted. They don't manufacture cricket balls in South America. (*Laughs again.*) First rate attorney: got him off. Caryl, will you excuse us?

CARYL *goes.* BILL *sits.*

SHELLY: She's becoming a joke.

BILL: I heard a joke about you. One of the new mod bands I was interested in – they came up to the office and on seeing a photo of you said: They used to guess when her albums would go platinum.

Now they ask if they'll go vinyl. (*Pause.*) I said in all honesty: if I thought they'd make one single to compare with your flops; if they could handle an audience like you; if they had a talent to endure like yours, I'd sign them immediately. I didn't.

SHELLY: The review in NME – Oedipus Rock –

BILL: He's a cunt.

SHELLY: I'll be forty in a couple of years.

BILL: And Bardot'll be fifty.

SHELLY: She's retired.

BILL: No performer ever retires. They just stop doing it for money.

Pause. SHELLY *puts on clown's red nose.*

SHELLY: When the day comes, I'll know.

BILL: Worry if ever the Val Doonican Show does an availability check.

SHELLY: Would you tell me?

BILL: Don't ask me questions like that.

ALUN *bounds on.*

ALUN: O fuck –

BILL: Good evening.

ALUN: Thank Christ you spoke – I'd have worried in case I put the wrong fucker on the fire.

BILL: I don't understand.

ALUN: Shelly –

BILL: Excuse us.

ALUN: I wanted –

BILL: In a few minutes, Alun.

ALUN *goes.*

Surely, as a friend – which I hope I am – there's someone you've got to see and I thought it would be better if you saw him on your own territory. And I brought him tonight because I couldn't get through to you to suggest this meeting.

SHELLY: Not tonight, Bill – I mean –

BILL: It's important. I'm afraid. What he wants to discuss with you he has said to me; I checked the details and he's no chancer trying to . . . I cancelled my vacation. You must see him and see if . . .

I can help. As a friend. His name is Mr Stanmore.

SHELLY: Who is he?

BILL: He'll explain. Mr Stanmore . . . Mr Stanmore . . . over here.

Pause. STANMORE, *dressed like a middle management executive, enters. He is slightly nervous.* BILL *goes.*

STANMORE: Are you Michelle?

SHELLY: What's left of her.

STANMORE: Michelle Maze, I mean?

SHELLY: Yes. The fireworks seem to have finished. There was supposed to be a grand finale. Perhaps the neighbourhood cats pissed on the blue paper.

STANMORE *is aware of their sharply different appearances.* SHELLY *removes her top hat. She holds it awkwardly.*

SHELLY: You never wear suits for work.

STANMORE: Well –

SHELLY: Labourers and bricklayers put on suits and ties at the drop of a hat. City gents wear casual clothes.

STANMORE: I was hoping we could talk . . . somewhere privately.

SHELLY: We are.

STANMORE: The house, perhaps.

SHELLY: I don't allow strangers in there. You're a stranger.

STANMORE: Well, here then.

SHELLY: Nothing wrong with the garden. I like the garden smells at night. They've just had the harvest round here. Can you smell the burned corn stubs?

She removes her clown's nose hurriedly.

STANMORE: Just the fireworks' sulphur, actually.

SHELLY: Are you a chemist?

STANMORE: By profession, I'm a tennis coach.

SHELLY: You don't look like one.

STANMORE: Ah, my business suit.

SHELLY: Is this a business meeting then?

STANMORE: I meant by that –

SHELLY: I'm an entertainer –

STANMORE: Yes, I know –

SHELLY: These clothes were to entertain –

STANMORE: I'm . . . (*Pause.*) This is more difficult than I had anticipated.

SHELLY: I'm a very busy person, you see –

STANMORE: This is crucial.

SHELLY: Bad news?

STANMORE: Yes, I'm afraid it is.

SHELLY: A death?

STANMORE: O, no – I don't know where to begin –

SHELLY: I don't with songs. Until I get a title. Would you like a drink?

STANMORE: Perhaps, a scotch –

SHELLY: No scotch. Only champagne. We've had a party. There's a dog end floating in it –

STANMORE: Ah –

SHELLY: It's filter tipped. They're less harmful to your health. What do you want then?

STANMORE: I expected you to be very aggressive and . . . I thought when I got out of my car, you'd stand out from everyone else. You're different, not what I'd been led to . . .

SHELLY: I thought tennis coaches were suntanned, always.

STANMORE: The club where I'm a pro, we have indoor courts.

SHELLY: I'm thinking of getting turf laid on the tennis court down there.

STANMORE: It's shielded from the wind. If you play a lot, Astro turf would . . .

SHELLY: Grass.

STANMORE: It wears out so quickly when a lot of people –

SHELLY: Not many people come here, Mr Stanmore.

STANMORE: You know my name. But you don't realise who I am. I'm married to Helen. The Helen that David married after you and he . . .

SHELLY: I heard she'd married again. I heard at about the same time I heard David had – they say a wife is always the last to know.

STANMORE: David always speaks – well of you.

SHELLY: You've met him then?

STANMORE: I had to – to . . . meet him.

SHELLY: And he spoke well of me?

STANMORE: Yes. He is . . . well, proud of your work. Follows your career with –

SHELLY: Does he still teach?

STANMORE: He makes his living painting now.

SHELLY: A decorator?

STANMORE: Painting pictures.

SHELLY: I never thought he'd stick with Helen. I never thought our kids would –

STANMORE: About –

SHELLY: You and her – get on?

STANMORE: Helen and me, we're very happy actually. And I get on well with the children and they give every indication of being . . . as you might say . . . with me. We live in Hove.

SHELLY: You and Helen have babies?

STANMORE: Three, actually.

SHELLY: Quite a handful.

STANMORE: Quite a handful.

SHELLY: My maintenance cheques – they adequate?

STANMORE: For *your* two children – yes. I don't earn much.

SHELLY: How long have you and Helen been married?

STANMORE: Twelve years. Two boys and a girl.

SHELLY: So – brothers as well as –

STANMORE: They get on well – until recently. Perhaps it's because he's the eldest.

SHELLY: I haven't seen him since he was eighteen months old.

STANMORE: When David and Helen made the adoption arrangements – they did as they thought best. I mean, you wouldn't co-operate at all and –

SHELLY: I found it too distressing. I

couldn't face all that. I never dreamed I'd lose my rights to see them again – my children.

STANMORE: I think it has been for the best. Since they were both so young when David and you – and since Helen and I intended to start a family. We're like one big happy family. They all look on Helen and me as their real parents.

SHELLY: And me? What about me, Mr Stanmore?

Pause.

STANMORE: We've never discussed you. I mean, they didn't know – which was probably not right. We'd put the children's interests first. We discussed all this and took advice from professional child psychoanalysts, whom Helen knows. And so it was a terrible shock –

SHELLY: When they find out who their real mother is –

STANMORE: We'd hoped they wouldn't –

SHELLY: They'll hate you. And David. He is so hard. I never saw him cry –

STANMORE: He's wept a great deal lately. As Helen has. As we all have. Since this . . . business with Billy came into the open.

Pause.

This boy . . . Billy. This son of yours.

Pause.

Helen discovered his diary. We have no idea how he found out you were his mother. And all that it has led to. In your hotel room in Brighton. And here.

Silence.

Psychologically, he's . . . well – it's shattering. The full realisation: the implications. The psychiatrist seems to think . . . it's not unheard of, in extremely backward families and in rural areas – however, this is a more complex case. And his age. He's supposed to be studying for 'O' levels. I'm not talking about the legal aspects, just his state of mind. His future. His sanity.

Pause.

Billy kept a diary. We were pleased he kept a diary. He began it before we went on holiday in Greece the preceding

summer. It was almost as if he wanted Helen to read it. He'd been quite hostile to her of late. Helen respected the boy's privacy, but we had been worried about Billy's changed attitude, his schoolwork, his staying out all night – the set he was in with. And so we discovered: by chance. Not at all night parties. But with you. His mother.

Pause.

The shock of the graphicness of his descriptions – of what he wrote. The vocabulary. The perversions. What you did to each other.

Pause.

I wouldn't mind killing you, quite frankly.

Pause.

We discussed it initially with David, since he and Helen had –

SHELLY: How much do they want?

Pause.

STANMORE: It's not a question of money. It's a question of Billy's state of mind –

SHELLY: How much do David and Helen want?

STANMORE: We thought, the best treatment available, whatever the cost.

SHELLY: This sounds business, not personal. You'd better make a deal with my manager, Bill.

STANMORE: Your son – for fuck's sake!

SHELLY: Bill can suggest good shrinks. Bill knows them all. Bill's been in rock 'n' roll for twenty-five years.

SHELLY *exits.*
Lights fade.
The sound of the band.

Berlin gig January 1980
Third quarter
Lights go up on the band. Instrumental until
SHELLY *enters and goes to the*
microphone. She is very demure.

SHELLY (*sings*): I'm a bad girl
    I gotta confess my sin
    Such a bad girl

Nobody knows just how bad I bin
I bin so bad my soul is running dry
Don't it bring the water to your eye?
I bin so bad I don't ever wanna die
Don't wanna know what's on the other
side of the sky.

I wanted you to know how I wanted you
so
But always ended up playing your games.
And so I lied behind your back
To cause you sorrow
To spite your face
To hurt and cause you pain.
As time goes by I've found
That sticks and stones can't hurt you
But wicked words still sicken in my mind.
The bruises go, the scars don't show when
you get older
But words destroy the face they left
behind.

I'm a bad girl
I gotta confess my sin
Such a bad girl
Nobody knows just how bad I bin
I bin so bad my soul is running dry
Don't it bring the water to your eye?
I bin so bad I don't ever wanna die
Don't wanna know what's on the other
side of the sky.

Fade lights and sound.

Act Four

The house; November 1979.
The sound of a passing train.
*The main room of the house. The furniture
is gone. There are dust covers on the large
table. It is bitterly cold.*
JOYCE *and* MAX *are removing crockery
from boxes. They wear coats, gloves etc.
They unwrap them from old newspaper.*
JOYCE *looks up and sees* SHELLY,
*looking white, in the Minstrel's Gallery.
She wears an overcoat, a woollen hat and a
blanket over her shoulders. She looks very ill
and still.*
Silence.

JOYCE: If you'll excuse me . . .

*She begins replacing newspaper in the
cardboard boxes.*

MAX: We were replacing the crockery. We
had no idea you were still here. We
understood from the new owner that you
had already vacated the property.
(*Pause.*) It was difficult to get in, even
with the keys. And the dust and the cold.
We thought you'd left weeks ago.

Pause.

Are you . . . unwell, Ma'am?

SHELLY *comes down from the gallery.
She has switched on Sibelius No.2. It
floods the room.
She slowly prowls round the table, fingers
a plate, looks at* MAX.

We packed them up. In storage. Until
such time. The new owner wanted us to
. . . get everything as it used to be. There
seems to have been a good deal of
furniture missing. Have you any idea
where . . . it is? (*Pause.*) These plates . . .
in fact, all the crockery were used more
for decoration than use. Mr Richardson
never used them. To eat from. Their
exquisite delicacy, you see. Are you
feeling ill, ma'am? We had no idea you
were still . . . here. The new owner, when
he employed us led me to believe the
house was vacant. Would you like us to
leave until you have . . . completed your
removing arrangements?

SHELLY *sits on the one chair at the head
of the table.*

SHELLY: Do you like Sibelius?

MAX: I respect the –

SHELLY: *Like*?

MAX: I'm not sure I'd know Sibelius' music –

SHELLY: This is it.

The tape stops.

MAX: Is there someone else in the house?

SHELLY: No. Sibelius' father wanted him to be a lawyer. Do law instead of music. If he'd done both! What a combination. No-one would have screwed him out of his house.

MAX: We understood from the new owner –

SHELLY: Is he English? Bill wouldn't sell to an Arab.

MAX: He's in industry. I think he manufactures buttons. We understood from him in fact you were . . . not in fact the owner but a tenant.

SHELLY: I owned the company which owned this house. It was a . . . all deals are complicated. I lost it.

MAX: This house?

SHELLY: You ought to be in rock'n'roll.

MAX: Well, I'm sure you'll be much happier in a different sort of house.

SHELLY: Brian Jones lived in the house where the bloke who wrote Winnie the Pooh wrote it.

MAX: I had no idea.

The tape starts again at the beginning of Sibelius' Second.

SHELLY: You *must* like this?

MAX: It would take some listening to. I have little appreciation actually of the techniques involved, the things one is supposed to appreciate in order to enjoy –

SHELLY: Just enjoy it!

MAX: I prefer songs, with words. I am most fond of Marlene Dietrich. Curiously.

SHELLY: Curiously?

MAX: I grew extremely fond of her singing 'Falling in Love Again'. Even during the war.

SHELLY: A great performer. She made the songs her own.

MAX: Precisely.

SHELLY: I wish I'd seen her.

MAX: I saw Dietrich the last time she appeared in London. Unforgettable. And seventy . . .

SHELLY: Ageless . . .

MAX: I think it was Hemingway: said, if she had nothing more than her voice she could break your heart.

SHELLY: Seeing her in performance – like seeing God. A performer.

MAX: My nephew spoke highly of your performances on stage.

Pause.

Some time after my wife and I moved from here, we were speaking to one of our nephews and quite by chance it came up, your name and our nephew revealed that he had been, and indeed still was, a keen admirer of yours. He has a collection of your records. A great fan, in fact. Of course, neither my wife nor I mentioned the circumstances of our leaving your employment. It would have . . . distressed him. He's got a family of his own now: twins; a quite pleasant modern house. They require such little housework.

SHELLY: Where does he live?

MAX: Nottingham.

SHELLY: We don't play Nottingham much, but when we next do –

MAX: O, he doesn't go to concerts now. He's too old. His children go. They're teenagers. (*Pause.*) Are you sure you're not unwell? So cold in here. You look . . . ill.

SHELLY *goes up. She switches off the tape. She looks down from the gallery.*

It took me quite by surprise, seeing you. Gave me quite a start. You see . . . in the village . . . there's talk of the accident yesterday. On the trainlines by the orchard. A scruffy person was killed, by a train. At first, from his description, so thin – we thought it was you. Long hair. And then my wife, she said, if it had been you there would probably have been a story about it in the Daily Telegraph. It's . . . well, that's why we were surprised to see you. Actually, so I heard, the young man was camping in the orchard. He was a vagrant. No-one knows who he was or where he came from. He frightened some children the other week; no it must have been last week. I brought the police with their dogs, on the new owner's behest. It was thought he might have been trespassing here, sleeping here. After the tragic accident, they found a sleeping bag in the orchard.

SHELLY *comes downstairs slowly.*

When do you think you might be leaving finally, ma'am?

SHELLY: Soonish. I'm off to Europe, maybe. I'm supposed to be.

MAX: Permanently?

SHELLY: I'm a gipsy, you know, really. A travelling minstrel. It was a mistake to try and 'bed down' here.

MAX: An Army phrase.

SHELLY: Royal Artillery, all those years. Do you miss it, Max, miss it?

MAX: Well, I sometimes think about the good times.

SHELLY: Where have all the good times gone? Eh? Eh? Do you miss them? Wish they could have . . . gone on, even now, still be going on?

MAX: Not especially. One feels most things one does have a purpose for, sometimes, quite a short period of time, and then when the usefulness is exhausted, one moves on.

SHELLY: You have been here thirty-five years.

MAX: I have a great feeling for this house. Its history, its beauty, its . . . the serenity of it. The fact that it has been standing here in England for five hundred years and will have been here for a thousand years probably, before . . . it ceases to leave a mark against the sky. On our afternoon strolls, as we come down from the forest, my wife always sighs a sigh of relief when we turn onto the bridle path: Ah, she says, *she's* still standing there.

Pause. SHELLY *walks a distance from* MAX *and with her back to him says:*

SHELLY: Have you ever tried to kill yourself?

Pause.

MAX: I'm sorry, I didn't quite catch that, what did you say?

SHELLY: I wondered, if you'd ever tried to kill yourself.

MAX: I can't imagine . . . what do you mean?

SHELLY: Suicide.

Pause.

MAX: Suicide? How do you mean, exactly?

SHELLY: Bad times. Very . . . low times. When you've been very down. Like in the war, everyone dying, friends dying, things smashing, all that misery. Pain. Wanted to die. To end . . . life.

MAX: There was always so much to hope for.

SHELLY: Not every day.

MAX: It seemed . . . indecent to despair. We took rather a dim view of pessimists.

Pause.

I don't understand such a question, really. I've never heard anyone mention it. I've read about people in the papers doing it. I couldn't understand the state of their mind.

MAX *looks at* SHELLY *anxiously.*

Are you all right, ma'am? Really?

JOYCE *comes in.*

JOYCE: I'm ready to go when you are Max.

She ignores SHELLY.

It's time we went back to the village. It's tea time.

MAX: In a moment, Joyce. I was . . . talking to our friend –

JOYCE: I'm cold.

MAX: Have you eaten anything . . . Michelle . . . here? Would you like a cup of tea perhaps?

JOYCE: I'm not making it. Not for her.

Pause.

MAX: Then I'll make it . . . if you'd like one?

SHELLY: I couldn't find anything . . . in the kitchen.

JOYCE: There isn't anything there. We had to clear it out. Wasn't that much there in the first place. I just bring enough for us to drink and some sandwiches, while we're working, clearing up the mess here. The mess.

MAX: Joyce, if you want to, walk on ahead. Some last minute arrangements I'm making with . . .

JOYCE: Don't do anything for her. She's a witch. She's filth. She's got no rights here. She shouldn't still be here by rights.

MAX: She looks as though she almost died –

JOYCE: Serve her right. All those disgusting things in the bedrooms. All the things that have happened there. The way she was to you.

SHELLY (*a whisper*): Sorry.

MAX: Parched –

JOYCE: Leave her. Leave her.

MAX: You almost died – didn't you?

JOYCE: Good. She shouldn't be here. She should never have been allowed here. Just thank God we'll never lay eyes on her again.

JOYCE *waits at the door for* MAX *who almost pleads.*

MAX: Something I can do for you –

Pause.

SHELLY: Just get that old cunt out of here.

Pause.
MAX *goes to* JOYCE. *He takes her bags.*

JOYCE: They'll send dogs in, to search the premises, for tramps. They might get you. You ought to go, go away, go where you're welcome. You're not welcome here.

SHELLY: Stay cool. You know, stay cool.

JOYCE *and* MAX *go out.*

I threw a firework party, you know. Everyone came, the village all came. Except you two.

The door bangs. SHELLY *goes to the table. She fingers a plate and just as we think she is going to smash it, she twiddles it on a finger, like a disc.*
She stares at it.
She sings in a thin voice:

SHELLY: With your long blond hair
And your eyes of blue

The only thing I ever get from you
Is sorrow, sorrow.

VAL *appears in the doorway: wrapped up in heavy winter clothes. She joins* SHELLY *in harmony.*

VAL/SHELLY: You're acting funny, spending all my money
You're out there playing
A high class game
Sorrow, sorrow.
I tried to find him
I couldn't resist him
I never knew how much I'd miss him –
Sorrow –

SHELLY: Sorrow.

Pause. SHELLY *sets down the plate with care.*

VAL: No-one was sure where you were. It's like an ice-box in here – Arctic.

Pause.

Just vanishing. Bill looked here weeks ago. You look terrible.

SHELLY: You look like Julie Christie in Doctor Zhivago.

VAL: Have you been here all the time?

Pause.

SHELLY: That was a good harmony, you know.

Pause.

VAL: Did the boy ever say to you . . .

Pause.

Your son . . .

Pause.

Bill thought perhaps I'd know something, could help. So he explained, confidentially. I haven't told anyone. Did the boy know?

SHELLY: I think so.

VAL: But he gave you no idea –

SHELLY: None. Funny, the first time I saw him he seemed familiar. Like Mandies are familiar . . . when you open a bottle . .

VAL: Are you all right?

SHELLY: I'm alive, you know.

VAL: Only just?

SHELLY: Alive. Blurred round the edges.

Survived the Mandies. I woke up. I was
. . . Alive.

VAL: I don't know how anyone is supposed
to cope with something like that. I
brought some coffee. And brandy.

She pours from a flask. SHELLY *drinks
from the brandy bottle.*

Bill did a deal with David and Helen.

SHELLY: 'The best lawyers.'

VAL: A French lawyer as adviser. Does
those non-property wedding contracts.
Apparently Bill bought their story – so he
owns the copyright. They can't sell it to
any newspapers. A watertight deal. They
can't hassle you again. He tried to phone
you.

SHELLY: The telephones are dis-
connected. The house is sold. Bill sold me
out.

VAL: He was very worried about you.

SHELLY: Suddenly very paternal.

VAL: Long time together. You were only
his second band.

SHELLY: A lot of groove cramming now.

VAL: He put his own money into you.

SHELLY: I never knew that.

VAL: The boys didn't know what to do.
The tour. Have you any idea what today
is? (*Pause.*) It's Christmas next week.
Then the tour starts; Brussels. (*Pause.*) If
you're in shape.

SHELLY: Same show for sixteen years. I
could do three quarters of it if I was deaf.

VAL: The new songs.

SHELLY: They're ordinary. Not any
nearer – the ideal.

VAL: Who is?

SHELLY: They say: everyone remembers
what they were doing, where they were,
the night they heard Kennedy had been
shot. Bullshit. Everyone knows where
they were, the night they first heard
Sergeant Pepper.

VAL: Yes –

SHELLY: I think the world is regressing.
Like unhappy, spoiled kids do. Go back
to when it was safe. That's why all the old
singles are getting played a lot again now.

VAL: You didn't know he was your son?

SHELLY: No.

VAL: You hadn't seen him for –

SHELLY: Since he was eighteen months old.

VAL: Well.

SHELLY: It's only a convention. Incest.
It's only like a social taboo. The Queen
doesn't invite you to her garden parties if
you fuck your own son. It was beautiful.
They made it dirty. They made it
disgusting. They were immoral. They
made money out of it.

Pause.

VAL: I drove here. I had a picnic on my
own. On the way here. I feel bad now –
not saving you food. It's good to be on
one's own –

SHELLY: The bad thing was –

VAL: What?

SHELLY: Pimm died last week. He was
here. I used to watch him through the
window. Up here, looked out, kept
seeing Pimm. He had a camp or
something. In the orchard. I thought I
was . . . hallucinating. He never came in.
Just kept looking up at the windows, from
a distance. Then I didn't see him. I heard
a commotion. The commotion when a
train stops in an emergency.

Pause.

Anyway, he's dead. Last week. I don't
feel anything. I think I haven't got any
feelings at all, to tell you the truth.
Because I didn't feel anything when I
never saw him again, staring up at the
window. At me. Woozy, woozy me.

Long pause.
*She takes rag-bandaged hand from under
the blanket.*

I don't think it's diseased. It doesn't hurt
and it isn't swollen. Maybe they disinfect
the guard dogs, so they don't give
criminals rabies.

Pause.

I was so out of my head in those days. The
stupid thing was: when I knew I'd been
made pregnant, I thought Pimm was
fucking me. I never wanted David's baby.
Babies. I would have wanted Pimm's.
Then.

She pauses: VAL *holds* SHELLY's *hand.*

I have self knowledge. I do. Fortunately I have a bad memory so I can tolerate it. (*Laughs.*) On my own here, you were the one person I wanted to sleep with. Did we? It feels as though we used to make it, but that time is so hazy. Can you stay with me for a while?

VAL *shrugs; smiles.*

Are they all incredibly mad at me?

Pause.

VAL: The boys weren't mad. They were worried. And hurt. It was their work as well.

SHELLY: After Pimm – I had to do someting physical, you see.

VAL: So you burned the master tape? The new stuff?

SHELLY: Was it any good then?

VAL: Three out of seven were great. Two very special.

SHELLY: All that work in the studio. All that . . . armoury. The Animals did 'House of the Rising Sun' in one take without even any double tracking. In fifteen minutes.

VAL: You sent a telegram saying sorry. Before anyone knew what you had done.

SHELLY: I got a reply from the President himself. New York City. 'A burned Angel is okay if it rises like a phoenix.' I thought that was very decent –

VAL: They *care* about you. They do.

Pause.

SHELLY: I wish my life could fit like cogs into someone's life and we'd run smoothly and happily together and separate for ever more. Will you stay with Mike?

VAL: I think after I get my degree, the kids'll be less of a handful – then I think I'll do my own thing. Leave him. Lead my own life. Like you.

SHELLY: I've been running my own . . . life, total freedom for sixteen years – fucked up.

VAL: You fucked it up yourself. No man did it for you.

SHELLY *drinks more.*

SHELLY: David didn't like this rock'n'roll lark at all, you know. I used to go crazy at him, like, after the work . . . after the work . . . his obvious, blatant boredom, with my friends, I accused him of losing friends for me. And all the time I was working, him alone, on his own, not making any. I kept his friends away, out of our rooms. I needed to sleep. We played some hefty old distances. This was in the beginning. A long time ago. I was so *hungry*. I wanted it so badly.

Silence.

People fell by the wayside. They still do. I mean, that's it basically. Pimm. I see Pimm, and a million headaches to fuck up me work, seen him. Let him wander off and . . . no work I wanted to do. Just empty ache for . . . Pimm not being around to fuck up . . . any more.

Pause.

I think regrets are quite valuable, actually, you know. I think if you go on regretting something that happened, it saves you getting involved in something new, another trauma, going through all that . . . upheaval in your head again. The downers. You know. And then again, like I wish I'd had someone . . . I cared about you . . . when I went down Bourbon Street, New Orleans. I dunno where the boys went . . . just bar to bar I went . . . the jazzmen in every bar, street schizzoid . . . beebop next to Dixieland and all the way up Bourbon Street. I got it on tape, would you like to hear it?

Pause. VAL *stands there.*

I resist anyone I might get mad about. I give them my phone number. I changed my phone number three times in the summer. Then I got embarrassed changing it, so I got some other phones, about five. And ansaphones. I felt . . . I got them away a bit. Then it's hard to get back. Like the audience . . . get them back, when you've started an hour late, you know. The first time we got to San Francisco, long delay, surprisingly small airport, really. Hot autumn night. Waiting for the baggage. There was a fault on the baggage tube or something. There was a guy standing talking to a cop; he was special for me. 20ish, thin bowling shirt; there was a breeze. The shirt blew about him a bit. He had nice hair. He stood in an open doorway staring at me. It could have been . . . for both of us.

VAL: It wasn't?

SHELLY: I never spoke to him. I was heavily into isolation at that time.

VAL: Playing to 20,000 a night in New York?

SHELLY: The bigger the gigs, the lonelier I feel. I think most people who come like them. And I err . . .

VAL: What?

SHELLY: I thought, the songs they all write to me about, identify with – the buzz I get when they say: 'That's me. How I felt. Feel. I'm not alone. You explained it, I couldn't.' And my 'scrapes'. This idea, I'm having these intensive uppers and downers, living fast life – on behalf of those whose lives are dull and mundane.

VAL: Well –

SHELLY: Dylan sang: Shouldn't let other people get your kicks for you. But I don't feel the big things any more. I get destroyed by the small things. The trivial. Nothing more trivial than a seven-inch band of black vinyl –

VAL: Potent – cheap music. We did.

SHELLY: What?

VAL: In bed. Fourteen years ago.

SHELLY: Was it any good?

They embrace.
BILL *appears on the gallery. The smell of his cigar smoke stops* VAL *and* SHELLY.

BILL: Business before pleasure. Thanks Val, for finding her.

VAL: Finding *Shelly*.

BILL: I said business before pleasure. Have you any personal things we can take back to London for you?

SHELLY: Records – letters – photos.

BILL: Val, please –

VAL: Where?

SHELLY: In the boiler-room. And my sleeping bag. And shoes. The Italian shoes and the cowboy boots.

VAL: I'll get them. And put them in my car. I'll wait outside for you.

VAL *goes.*

BILL: I was worried about you.

SHELLY: Were you?

BILL: I was.

SHELLY: I – didn't want to deliberately –

BILL: I can't hear you. I'll come down.

SHELLY: O.

Pause.
BILL *is now on the ground.*

BILL: This barn – you made a profit on the sale.

SHELLY: I didn't want to sell.

BILL: You'd die here. You need a permanent hotel suite in London. New York, maybe Paris – or –

SHELLY: Not a house?

BILL: Would Val make you happy?

SHELLY: Mike is a flabby guitarist.

BILL: Get a younger guitarist. A looker. Very young, hungry –

SHELLY: When the lights are red, on stage I leap around like a seventeen year old.

BILL *laughs and hugs her. He produces an album from his briefcase.*

BILL: Your new album. Out in time for the tour. Avoided Christmas – albums get lost. January, good month. Heavy promotion. People like some real rock'n' roll after all those stupid Christmas songs.

SHELLY: Our third 'Greatest Hits' album.

BILL: Your first for five years. A great photo.

SHELLY: Just me?

BILL: You objecting?

SHELLY: This our new album?

BILL: You burned the master tape. We need it for the tour.

SHELLY: Tour?

BILL: Two months. Forty-five venues. And ending with three nights in Berlin.

SHELLY: O.

BILL: Starting Wednesday after Christmas.

SHELLY: I'm out of shape. I . . . I'm out of

form.

BILL: Listen to the album. A cassette here – play it in the car on the drive to London.

SHELLY: I can't believe in these songs any more.

BILL: You made them very personal.

SHELLY: That was years ago!

BILL: I still believe in it. You still follow it through.

SHELLY: Singing the same songs for sixteen years – night after night. I might as well be a boring filing clerk.

BILL: Want to make a swap with one?

SHELLY: There isn't enough time to rehearse.

BILL: I got three 'live' rehearsals. Tomorrow night, then Friday, then Saturday. Pulled out a young newish mod band I'm testing. You replace them to feel your way back. Rehearse over Christmas. Then Brussels –

SHELLY: How do you mean live rehearsals?

BILL: Three gigs. At University 'hops'. Students. Red brick low brow university gigs. They'll be expecting a mod band and get you. They'll be livid. They're so serious, so image, so careeristic. You'll hate them. Hate them like poison. So you'll be fantastic.

SHELLY: I work best on hate.

BILL: That's why we keep Caryl.

SHELLY: I work best – on hate.

BILL: Pimm's guitar solos sound wonderful. (*Looking at the album cover.*) Five credits. His photo at the back.

SHELLY: He's dead.

BILL: He was on schedule. A tragedy. A waste.

SHELLY: Such a waste.

BILL: All your energy! And no direction.

SHELLY: That's why. No purpose. That's why –

BILL: Why?

SHELLY: Why I'm in rock'n'roll.

BILL: Yes. And on the road.

She goes. BILL *watches her go.*
Fade light.
Fade in crowd sounds.

Berlin gig.
Last quarter.
Bright coloured lights.
An instrumental of rock. Then SHELLY *comes on.*

SHELLY: Well, this is the end then. Thank you for being so nice and polite and falling asleep quietly. No wonder Marlene Dietrich never married a Kraut. I got to remind you to thank the band . . . danke . . . danke . . . Steve . . . he has problems too you know. Alun . . . he only drinks because he doesn't like his guitar playing. Howard . . . he's all right. Mick . . . his wife wants to make me. . . There's a guy in Berlin here in a pharmacy who leaves pills and terrible bad, dangerous junk in our bedrooms . . . that could cause bad problems for a lot of people. The last time here a guy in our band got it very bad because of the fucking murdering pharmacy bastard. Eight years ago. He ain't with us any more. You can hear him on records. He didn't make enough. He never got to do what he wanted to do. Like I do. Goodnight then. Believe in the music. It'll get you through. We've been through a stormy time. But we've made it to the other side. With, so far, only one casualty. This is the one we never did when he was here. This is for Pimm.

The lights go to red.

When the night, has come, and the land is dark
And the moonlight, is the only light you see
Then I won't be afraid,
O no I won't be afraid,
Just so long, as you stand by me.

The lights slowly fade during the last verse.

When the sky that we look upon should tumble and fall
And the mountains should crumble to the sea
I won't cry, I won't cry,

No I won't shed a tear
Just so long as you stand by me
Stand by me,
Stand by me,
Stand by me.

Just a light on her face.
No light left.

IT'S A ROCK 'N' ROLL NIGHT TONIGHT

BAD GIRL BLUES